FLIRTING IN SPANISH

Praise for *Flirting In Spanish*

"Running from paralyzing memories…[the author] lands in Mexico at 32, trying not to fall for a much younger local. **When she finally achieves hard-won contentment, it's a joyous moment.**"

— *Publishers Weekly.*

"Susan McKinney has a real story to tell, both fraught and magical, and she knows how to tell it. *Flirting in Spanish* will take you places you've likely never been, and you will emerge amazed and illuminated."

— Tony Cohan, author of *Mexican Days* and *On Mexican Time.*

"An improbable yet transcendent and touching love story, with love crossing and conquering language, cultural, class and social barriers. Along the way we are treated to a revealing inside glimpse of working-class Mexican family life through the eyes of a privileged American woman who sacrifices everything for love and, by doing so, regains her life."

— Rick Skwiot, Hemingway First Novel Award author of *Death in Mexico.*

"Susan McKinney has an amazing tale to tell about moving from one culture to another, out of her comfort zone and into a colorful new kind of happiness."

— Laura Fraser, author of *All Over the Map* and *An Italian Affair.*

"Captivating, moving and enlightening."

— Sandra Gulland, international bestselling author of *The Josephine B Trilogy* and *Mistress of the Sun.*

"Told with heart and pizzazz, a true life story you will not be able to put down."

— Beverly Donofrio, author of *Riding in Cars with Boys* and *Looking for Mary.*

FLIRTING IN SPANISH

What Mexico taught me about
love, living and forgiveness

BY

Susan McKinney de Ortega

ANTAEUS BOOKS

ISBN 978-0-9828591-9-3
Library of Congress Control Number: 2011906131

Book design by Amy McAdams
www.amymcadams.com

www.FlirtingInSpanish.com

www.AntaeusBooks.com

For Carlos,
still my novio

More than talent, a winner needs drive,
determination and desire.

Former NBA coach Jack McKinney

CONTENTS

Prologue

PART I
Naked
Maestra
Bimbo
Kiss
Familia
Promenade
Dating Mexican Men
Thanksgiving
Love Letters in the Sand
Hairnet
Bad Neighborhood
The Lamina-Roofed House
La Chiona
Lights in the Corner
I Love Lucy
Runaway
Two Red Lines
In the Locker Room
Black Eye
Defended
You Are My Sunshine
Jailed

PART II
I Can't Stop Looking at Her
Escape
Ninety-Dollar Apartment
Family Reunion
2010

Glossary of Common Spanish Phrases

PREFACE

While memory and a memoir are highly personal and subjective, I've done my best here to tell the truth about a crucial phase of my life. And while it's true that I went to San Miguel de Allende and met a poor Mexican teenager, some of the events in this book have been a bit time-squished to keep the narrative flowing. But in the emotional truth—for me, the loftier goal of a memoir—there is no fudging. I fell hopelessly and utterly in love, doubted myself and then, made a decision. The emotional truth at the core of the story is unaltered.

I have changed the names of many people depicted in this memoir. But Carlos, Carla and Sean are the real names of my husband, and my two beautiful Mexican-American girls.

FLIRTING IN SPANISH

PROLOGUE

It is an October night in 1992 and, despite the chill in the air outside, I am wearing a sleeveless powder blue velvet top with front darts atop my low slung black jeans. My clothing choice would be vintage and hip in downtown Philadelphia where I routinely roamed four months prior, but here in a discothèque in the heart of central Mexico, the irony is lost and I suspect I even look a bit old-ladyish. Around me, Mexican adolescents dressed in shiny pants, short skirts and high heels shimmy to the disco beat, but I have stopped noticing the teens because I am kissing one with my eyes closed.

His name is Carlos, and he is my 19 year-old student and I have tried to resist him because I am the teacher, but not really. I haven't been trying to resist him at all; I've only told myself so. If I had, I wouldn't have agreed to come out with him on a Sunday night, when the disco closes earlier than other nights so it seems more innocent. I have brought along my teacher friend, Gussie, to pretend to myself I am not going out with a student, but the ruse is rapidly falling away. Muted squares of light from the disco ball above fall across our faces and Cristian Castro is singing, "Babe, I love you so. And I want you to know. That I'm going to miss your love, the minute you walk out that door." Then he sings, "Please don't go. Don't gooooo. Don't go away." And there is a deep sadness to the words already, because I have been asking myself in the cooler days of October why I am still in Mexico. I am a 33-year old coach's daughter, teaching English a few hours a week for less than minimum wage, and it is something, but not much, so I also ask, not only for how much longer will I stay, but what would be my destination should I leave. And now I am kissing my student and the questions will never be asked in a carefree way again.

But tonight, under the glittering disco ball, shuffling in a small circle on a wooden floor, one arm delicately around Carlos' shoulder, the other hand clutching the too-long sleeve of his paisley button-down shirt, realizing his lips are so soft because he has almost no facial hair, I am not thinking of my life's direction or lack thereof. I am just *una muchacha besando a un muchacho*, not wanting the song or the kiss to end.

PART I

NAKED

Outside the studio window I gazed through from my platform, a hummingbird dipped its beak into the orange bell of a *llamarada*. I was naked. My head looked to the right; my left arm held my weight; my right hand was on my hip. My nose was itchy, but I dared not move. My five dollars an hour depended on it.

In a circle around me, twelve heads bent over sketch paper. A guy in a safari hat looked at me through a square he made with his charcoal-blackened thumbs and forefingers. I was used to being stared at. I'd been modeling twice a week for a month, ever since I realized the dollar bills I had stuffed between the pages of *The Lawless Roads*, and changed periodically at the Casa de Cambio on Calle Correo, were almost gone.

Up on the platform, I was thinking about when I used to be Somebody. When I was a television news reporter, holding a microphone and saying, "school board... snow removal budget... dairy price supports... hundred-year old barn, Susan McKinney, News 3." A Torch-Runner to light the fire to start the Madison Olympics. A Proud Little Girl opening to the sports pages first thing Sunday morning to see my father's name. The Coach's Daughter cruising the streets of Portland, Oregon on the back of a convertible, showered with confetti and roses after the Trailblazers won the NBA championship. Now after being the Girl Who Traveled to Mexico for the Summer, I was the Girl Who Took her Clothes off for Five Dollars an Hour. I wished somebody would suggest going for a beer, so I could forget about The Question. Should I leave Mexico in September, or should I stay and continue to search for who I was?

Months before my arrival in San Miguel, my grandfather had died, leaving me a thousandaire. It seemed a sign. I could actually get away, not work for once in my life, and write my book. After my summer lease was up, I'd go back to Philadelphia—that was the plan. But, now, gazing out the window at sights that had become familiar—the sharp blue sky that artists came to paint, the startling texture of an eroding centuries-old wall, the tiny hummingbird, who the Maya considered to be the "sun in disguise,"— returning to a bartending job didn't have the urgency it once did.

After three months in Mexico, I had a couple of friends, all of whom seemed to have settled for life without a lot of expectations. Jim, the art gallery curator at El Instituto Allende, rented a little house for $100 dollars a month. He painted in that house, ran the gallery at El Instituto and took on one poetry student at a time for classes he gave at his gallery desk. His present student had Buddy Holly eyeglasses and a lot of 20-year old angst.

Claudia, the other American model, was my age. She'd come to San Miguel with a boyfriend, who'd dumped her when they blew through all of her money. She existed on spaghetti, a secret savings the ex-boyfriend hadn't known about, and modeling jobs, not unlike me. The artists studying at El Instituto, mostly Americans, liked to draw a regular named Luz, who had mountains of flesh and a handsome Aztec face, but the instructor, Ted, preferred to hire Claudia and me because we showed up. When Luz couldn't make her modeling gigs, she sent her 9-year old son in her place.

Sketch paper was rustling, and Ted was doing a little thing with his finger that meant I was to take another pose. I put one foot in front of the other, left pointing west, right going east. I held my hands as if I were cupping a large egg below my navel, a pose my body still remembered from fifth grade in Miss Ellen's Ballet class. I was my own metaphor, unclothed and unmoving, ready to be redefined.

For the next twenty minutes, I tried to think only of the *cafecito* I would order from El Instituto's café, whitened with cream from a can.

"You know, I had a dream last night," I said to a drawing student from Nashville during the break. His white T-shirt never got dirty no matter how much charcoal he smudged on his tortilla paper.

"There was a baby," I said.

"New beginnings," said Nashville. "Hey, we're going to meet in the Jardín tonight around seven, and then do some partying. Like, maybe at Carmen's place. Or yours?" His eyebrows went up.

My place was a casita with goatskin rugs, owned by the people who'd written *A People's Guide to Mexico*, the RV and camping guide that advised what to do for a hangover. *The standard Mexican remedy is to continue drinking.* It was on a quiet street and the neighbors had not called the cops on the previous get-togethers I'd had. But I was in a brooding mood, thinking of the dream.

In my casita-hideaway, I often sat under the eucalyptus tree in my yard for hours, reading, thinking and dozing. Once my next-door neighbor, a lady who wore a rebozo over her head, invited me into her house to give me limes. A door led from her front room, which was bare except for holy cards and candles, into her yard. She'd washed her dishes at an outdoor sink, and hung them on some bushes to dry. My little world felt intensely private right now. I wasn't up to hosting the Hacky Sack and patchouli crowd. "Not my place," I said.

Nashville made a pouty face. I sighed. Maybe it was time to go home, meet some Philadelphia lawyer and try to imagine a picket fence.

Back in the drawing studio, students were taking their places again. I pulled my dress over my head and climbed onto the platform. My fellow model, Claudia meditated. It was something I'd always thought I'd do, but I was still struggling to see the point. I mean if you're going to sit still, you might as well read a book. Or if I needed a break between writing chapters, I went for a run. Plus, although frightening memories of the 1980 incident had faded, sometimes, if I sat quietly long enough, they intruded. Yet, I'd been in Mexico for three months, had adjusted to less *prisa,* hurry, and more space in my head and I hadn't been overwhelmed with the urge to run, as had been my pattern. Wasn't that a good argument to stay?

Here I was, sitting still for another hour, so I closed my eyes and tried to think of nothing. And of course I thought of my father, who at my age, had chalked up a 17-9 Win/Loss record at St. Joseph's College. He'd, ho-hum, won the Gator Bowl Tournament at Christmas and gotten the team into the NCAA post-season tournament at season's end.

I, at age 33, had decimated whatever savings I'd once had and was scrounging for rent and food money. At noon, when my three-hour session was over, I would take home about fifteen dollars. The 1977 NBA championship ring my father wore was worth 15-*thousand* dollars.

When the students rolled up their butcher paper filled

with drawings of me and wiped off their blackened fingers, I headed out. As I was about to pass under El Instituto's high doorway, Ted hurried up and stopped me.

"Jim," he said, meaning our painter friend who ran the Instituto's gallery. "They found him dead at his easel in his house yesterday."

My hand flew to my mouth. So much for new beginnings.

"The American Consul is trying to find family members in the States. Jim's at the cemetery. Once someone is notified, he can be buried."

Twenty minutes later, I was walking along the Ancha de San Antonio with Ted and his wife, Kelly, headed toward the edge of town to the *panteon*. We waved down an aproned lady with a bucket of flowers on her head and dug coins out of our pockets. Kelly pointed to some orange lilies. The lady swung the bucket to the ground, separated a handful, and tied the bunch with a long piece of grass.

A white iron gate guarded the entrance to the *panteon*. Across the street, a lone sno-cone seller awaited visitors. His flavors were lined up in old Coke bottles in an oversized basket on the front of his three-wheeled bike.

Inside, gravesites were riots of color—blue painted structures like doll houses topping tombs, pink carnations, and creamy calla lilies. Somebody had left a bottle of tequila by the headstone of Senor Umberto Rodriguez who was Beloved by His Children and Grandchildren (I was able to translate).

I peeked into a windowless concrete room to the right and saw a casket on rolling legs.

"That's heem," said Rodrigo, another San Miguel artist who'd heard the news. Behind him came an American woman who made art from chicken bones, and Gina, who also taught art at El Instituto.

"They can't put him into the ground until they can

notify family," Ted informed the group. We looked at the sky, at the gravesites, at our feet. The sno-cone seller outside jingled his bell.

Then Gina said, "Anybody got any mescal?" and people laughed. Rodrigo offered Faros cigarettes, and Gina took one.

"Maybe everyone can say a few words about Jim," Ted suggested.

"Jim liked to party," Gina said. Gina likes to party, I thought. It was funny how we saw ourselves reflected in others.

"Jim died doing what he loved," I said. "I'd be happy if some day that can be said about me."

When the sun was dropping behind the trees and nobody had shown up, I asked, "What happens if they can't find any family members?" There didn't seem to be any refrigeration.

Rodrigo shrugged. I stood and wandered into the holding room and that's when I noticed Jim had company—two bullet-ridden bodies—one on a raised slab, covered by sheet except for a bloody patch of black hair; the other a woman, lying uncovered on the concrete floor. She was about my age, wearing a dress, an apron and dusty patent leather shoes. Her only distinguishing mark was a round, black hole in her forehead. She was surrounded by votive candles.

Life was so raw in Mexico. I gazed at Jim's coffin next to the lady with the bullet hole, both waiting to be claimed. Jim had been painting one minute, keeled over onto the floor the next. Alone. I didn't want that to be me.

I went back to the gravesites. Everyone was sitting on the ground. Someone had produced a bottle of Don Julio and a few plastic cups. Rodrigo held a Faros between his thumb and forefinger. Gina was telling a story. People were sipping the tequila and laughing. Jim would have liked it.

My friends scooted over, and I sat in their circle under the shrimp-colored sky.

"My husband thought my boobs were *his*," said Gina.

"*Ex*-husband," reminded the bone artist.

Everyone had a story. I did too. Mine included an NBA player who'd attacked me, thinking I was a fly—the word my mother and my sister and I used for the girls who clustered around the locker room doors in all of the National Basketball Association cities, waiting for the players to come out, waiting to be chosen. The Player hadn't realized I was the coach's daughter, a girl who had always enjoyed protection and respect. He hadn't taken no for an answer. The next day, his Agent had called. If I ever spoke about it, my father, then the Lakers coach who'd fallen from a bicycle and remained in a coma for three weeks, would never work in the NBA again. That was the part of my story I didn't want to see when I closed my eyes. The part that had made me think real boyfriends who had Sunday brunch with you were for other girls, and that one night stands with busboys was all I could expect for myself. The part that made me run from city to city and finally travel on an overnight bus into the heart of Mexico.

Rodrigo handed me a cup of tequila. I lifted my head and drank. Shoo to the girl who hadn't moved past her fear and shame. *That* girl could stay with the gravesites and the ghosts. That part of my story wasn't the only thing about me. I was moving on. I said these words to myself: I am ready for anything.

///

I tucked all the money I had left in the world into my jeans pocket and set out.

It was Monday. Sunday was a drinking day for many Mexican workers. Sunday had obviously been hard on a guy I found passed out, facedown on the dirt road shortcut to the Central de Autobuses. As I stepped around him, and looked for a cop to inform, a writer I knew named Barb waved and hurried toward me. Barb's hair stuck out like baby bird fuzz around her head. She'd shaved it after a fight with her American boyfriend.

"We're going to Arizona!" Barb panted, reaching me. "Andrew wants to leave a replacement for himself at Prepatoria El Pipila. It's a high school up from the Pemex station."

"So you and Andrew made up."

"Yeah." She shrugged.

"I've never taught before," I said.

"You speak English, don't you? You're a writer? You must know something about words."

So instead of buying a bus ticket to the border, I went home, put on a skirt and headed for the high school. Once when I was a news reporter, I had had a college intern trail me around all day, learning the ropes. I was thinking about how to make that sound like teaching experience as I passed kids with piles of notebooks lounging on the school's stone wall on my way to the principal's office.

"You can take all the afternoon classes?" was all the director asked me. He was about my age, one of the few men I'd seen in San Miguel wear a tie. When I got my journalism degree from the University of Wisconsin, I'd never imagined explaining English verbs to Mexican teens. The director offered five dollars an hour.

I became an English teacher.

MAESTRA

In the plain concrete classroom, a wolf whistle broke the deadly calm. My hand, writing with chalk at the blackboard, stopped. I was suddenly conscious of the seat of my jeans hugging my ass. "E-Y" I wrote. "McKinney," I said, turning around.

Eighteen Mexican teens stared at me.

"Here are some word cards," I said in English, shuffling the stack so nobody would notice my trembling hands.

"You say the English word first, then the Spanish," I explained. "Let's do it with a partner."

Nobody moved. Where were the serious eagerly-taking-down-my-every-word students I'd dreamed of? What was with these bored expressions on boys who looked like they'd begun shaving only weeks before? Before class, the director had explained that most students in Mexico only completed grade school. A smaller percentage went to middle school, and if an individual actually finished high school and had some English language skills, life offered many opportunities.

"It is very important that these students learn English," the director told me sternly.

"Come on," I chirped. "Try it. Sky. *Cielo*. Sky." I turned to write *sun* on the board and felt the room grow still again. I heard a girl snicker. A manly snort answered her derisive laugh. It was my first day.

If I cried, they'd know I'd never taught before. I lowered the hand that gripped the chalk. I would turn slowly from the blackboard, I told myself, walk out in a dignified manner and never return. I would go back to Philly and bartend.

I smelled chalk dust and heard heels clicking across the floor of the next classroom. I'd seen the other teacher arrive wearing a skirt to her knees, purposely carrying a load of books. I wore Levis and had debated my footwear – motorcycle boots, Doc Martens or leather sandals? The classroom was hot, the air still. I was glad I'd decided on sandals.

I took a breath and forced a steely look into my eyes. "How old are you people anyway?" I said, turning around. The students stopped laughing. I had never run away from difficult situations before. I'd met television, magazine and advertising deadlines. I'd handled twenty bar customers at a time. I knew how to work under pressure. I folded my arms and stood with my legs apart, like my father with his whistle around his neck.

"*Cuantos años tienen*? We'll learn this. Everybody say it. How old are you?" I pointed my finger into the nose of a kid with stubby chin hairs.

"Veinte."

"Twenty," I said. I stood with my finger in his face until he mumbled "Twenty."

Nineteen, sixteen came the answers in Spanish. Eighteen, fifteen, seventeen, twenty-two.

One, two, three I wrote on the board. "O.K.," I said.

"We'll begin with numbers."

After class, boys surrounded my desk. "Maestra, cuantos años tiene Ud.?" asked a pimply kid in Spanish. "How old are you?"

"I'm thirty-three years old," I replied, mindful of the phrases we'd practiced.

"Where are you from? Are you married? Why aren't you married? Want to marry me? Don't you have children? *Vive Ud. sola?*"

Now that they were close, I could see I was right—some of these kids were barely out of middle school. I said I lived alone. Boys elbowed each other and raised their eyebrows. "Can I come to your house?"

Where were the eager kids who were grateful to see a genuine English speaker behind the desk? Was I in a classroom being *hit* on?

The next day after class, a kid who looked to be about sixteen tucked his hands behind the multicolored suspenders attached to his jeans and said in Spanish, "Teacher, can I come to your house and practice speaking English?"

To my *house*? They were no different than the rich guys in the bars—chatting up the American girls because they thought we were easy.

"When you can read an entire page of Shakespeare to me out loud, you can come to my house," I said. The kid furrowed his eyebrows, snapped his suspenders and left. I was gathering my books into a pile when I noticed that one boy remained, still seated at the second desk in the middle row, watching me.

Carlos. I remembered his name because I'd noticed him. He'd stood back while the other boys fired questions at me. The black sunglasses he'd worn the entire hour were off now.

"Ever taught before?"

Was I that obvious? "No," I sighed.

Carlos' thick, midnight-black hair was cut short in the back and on the left side. The rest of his hair fell in a long sheet from his part down to his chin on the right side, like some punk wannabe without tattoos or attitude.

"Where do you live?" Carlos asked.

"Over the river and through the woods," I mumbled.

Carlos was looking at me patiently.

"Sorry," I sighed.

"They're just testing you to see if you're like the vacation girls that arrive here in the summer."

"What are the vacation girls like?" I asked distractedly, hoisting my stuffed backpack onto my shoulder. I knew the vacation girls – shrieky and loud and hung-over. Out in the bars until three A.M., morally on vacation from the correct behavior they exhibited in their towns the other fifty-one weeks of the year.

"Easy."

"It's popular to make assumptions about American women, I see."

"I don't make assumptions about people I don't know. It's just that sometimes that's true."

How do you know? I wanted to retort. How many have you picked up? But I didn't want him to think I cared. We were in the school hall now. Without breaking step, Carlos had slipped my backpack off my shoulder and lifted it onto his. He kept walking. I hurried to catch up.

How old did he say he was? I thought back to his answer to the age exercise the day before. Nineteen. He was nineteen years old.

///

It was the second week and I walked up and down the aisles, feeling teacherly. The students were writing verbs in simple sentences on sheets I'd made up and photocopied since not a single student bought the book I told them to buy. Carlos had almost finished the exercise, I saw, passing his seat, while other kids looked around, clueless. With my finger, I touched a cross of string and black beads he wore at his throat.

"That's very nice," I whispered.

"My sister made it," he said and smiled at me.

I smiled, and then feeling foolish, looked up. The class had dwindled to some ten students who showed up regularly. All of them were looking at me.

I moved on, shocked at my own recklessness, holding my hands together to stop them from shaking. I went to the blackboard to hide my face, picked up chalk, couldn't think of what to write.

Carlos was sitting on the low wall as I left the building. He hopped off and hurried towards me. Removing the cross from his neck in one quick motion, he placed it over my head. My heart raced, my cheeks burned. There were a hundred kids around us. Carlos flashed me a Tom Cruise smile and disappeared.

I walked to the street. *Get a grip*, I told myself, feeling the ghost of his hands where they had floated past my head and lightly touched my shoulders.

Heads bent over papers, pens busily scratched. The students were writing lists of ten words they would like translated into English.

During the break, I looked at the papers. One girl, who wore neon orange lipstick and yelled across the room to her friends, wrote *pintar*, then the words for paintbrush, pencil, pastel, charcoal, form, shade, art, haircut, love. I pulled out Carlos' sheet. Juan Carlos Ortega Moreno. His list read: copper, brass, to sand, to shine, to paint, to play basketball, to score, to rebound, to admire and *vieja con bonita figura*. Girl with a good figure! How idiotic, how *infant*! That's it, I resolved. I'm over my fascination with this pretty boy, because that's all he is—a boy. Girl with a good figure! Could anything be more immature? I shoved his paper to the bottom of the pile.

Carlos came to my desk after class and told me, "We go dancing at Laberintos on Sunday nights. You should come."

"No, thank you," I said primly. "I can't." I was the teacher, after all. I felt a flutter of excitement inside and pretended I didn't.

In my casita, I soaked vegetables in purified water. I made a salad and poured olive oil over it. I looked at the memoir about being the coach's daughter I'd come to compose, thought of writing a few sentences, didn't. I drank a cup of tea and went to bed. I touched the black cross; fell asleep with it in my fingers, feeling how it lay at my throat.

Carlos sat in front of me in a pair of overall shorts. The entire room was taken up by his bare legs. All through my childhood, my father's basketball teams had sat on benches in shorts, legs casually spread, completely owning their space. I'd had a crush on each and every player—men who, like my father, looked as if they owned the world.

When I looked up from my verb sheet, I could see nothing but smooth brown skin, strongly muscled calves covered by sparse, manly black hairs! I caught my breath and turned away. I felt like I was spying on him in the shower. *Fool*, I said to myself.

A week later, Carlos waited in the classroom while the others filed out. "We're going dancing at Laberintos on Sunday," he said. "Why don't you come?"

"Of course not," I said disdainfully. Who does he think he is, asking out the teacher! Expecting me to go! Then I thought, *who's we?* I thought, *what a beautiful face.*

"I can't. My mother is coming. I'm going to Mexico City right now to pick her up." I snapped a book shut. Then I continued, against my will. "Do you make things in metal?"

"Boxes, frames, mirrors and stuff." He laughed. "I've worked in my brother-in-law's brass and tin *taller* since I was eleven. It's not like *I* make the items. I might hammer star patterns into a hundred lamp shades."

I'd seen those workshops on walks through the neighborhoods – unfinished rooms, blow torches, tree stumps for work tables, young guys pounding patterns into sheets of tin with primitive tools. I imagined him bent over with a hammer, concentrated.

"Do you paint?"

"When nobody is looking. I bought a gourd in the market yesterday. That's the next thing I'm going to paint. I've painted on straw mats, scrap wood, my brother's pants. Yesterday I added the Virgen de Guadalupe and a dozen roses to the leg of his jeans. We'll see how he makes me pay when he finds out. Ha! Well, gotta go," Carlos said, and walked to the door. When he turned back, I was still watching him.

I exited the school building. My toothbrush was packed in the overnight bag on my shoulder. As I headed down the hill, toward the bus station, I heard footsteps. Carlos ran after me, his black flag of hair flapping. Reaching me, he held out his hand. I held out mine and Carlos dropped a shiny brass pocket mirror that opened like a book into it. While I gazed at it, he turned and ran back up the hill again. I stuck the mirror in the inside pocket of my vintage blazer, and touched it as the bus rumbled out of San Miguel.

BIMBO

"Your hair looks nice," my mother said. We wheeled her spotless American Tourister luggage across the Mexico City Marriott lobby, until a uniformed bellhop appeared and took the suitcase handles in his gloved hands. The valet stepped into a chrome elevator, and held the door back while we passed.

My hair looked awful. In the elevator mirrors, I could see how shapeless it had gotten. Plus the platinum color was growing out, giving me a skunky look. San Miguel dust still clung to my Doc Martens.

In my mother's room, I eyed the brocade bedspread and mahogany table and decided the only place for my backpack, which I hadn't noticed was scruffy until now, was the floor. I rooted in the mini-bar, and then saw the prices noted on a card above and put my mineral water back. At the window, I stared at the fashionable Polanco district spread in a grid of museums and boutiques below.

"How's teaching?" my mother asked. In crackling phone calls to my mother from San Miguel's long distance *caseta*, I'd fielded questions about salary and living conditions, then usually pretended I was losing the connection and hung up. Teaching made me think of Carlos. Carlos in his loose jeans, his barrio haircut—I shook my head.

"Teaching is good," I said. Teaching was respectable. I looked to see if my mother felt soothed, but she was pacing. "I better check and see if the bathroom is clean," she said.

"Mom, this is a Marriott."

My mother was looking me up and down. I didn't own an iron, and I couldn't afford dry-cleaning; I guessed it showed.

"Let's go find something to eat, Ma," I said.

Before we knew it, the hotel people had whooshed us into a black Lincoln that charged $20 dollars to deliver us to a pink and yellow restaurant two blocks away. Gay sombreros and small painted guitars hung on the walls. A hurried waiter banged tortilla chips down on our table. "What kind of tequila you want?" he asked in English. Competing bands of mariachis roamed the cavernous room.

"What's Dad doing these days?" I asked, after we'd ordered chicken *mole* from the oversized menu.

"Working with some kid over in Atlantic City who wants New York to draft him."

"And you, Mom?"

"I'm trying out for *Fiddler on the Roof*. I want to be the mother but they want me to be the matchmaker."

"Matchmaker! Ha! What a stretch! You never liked anyone I dated."

"That's not true."

"Who did you like?"

"Hm. Not Ed Rosen who hung Bill up by his belt loop on the wall."

"That was high school. I only wanted to have a boyfriend."

"Not that college guy." Scott—she knew his name. "You always had dark circles under your eyes when you came from college."

"Maybe that was from exams."

"We both know it wasn't." My mother sipped a margarita. "After college, you didn't seem interested in dating, did you?"

Here was my chance. I could tell her about the Player and the Agent and then she would understand why I hadn't managed to keep a relationship together. My heart started doing its Sam the Drummer thing – banging like it was being hit by the fanatic St. Joe's student who beat a drum during all my dad's college games.

"There was a reason I didn't date much, Mom."

"Yeah, nobody was good enough for you, right? I'd see men interested in you and you didn't seem to *notice.*" Mom dipped a chip in the salsa. "The last nice boyfriend you had was when you were in high school."

"Russell," I sighed. Russell, the Whitefish Bay basketball, tennis and volleyball star.

"What about now?"

Carlos' face popped up in my mole sauce. Nineteen, hadn't finished high school. Ha.

"Mom, I'm in Mexico."

"There are no men in Mexico?"

I shrugged.

"Come on home then. Rose O'Donnell's son asks about you. He's a golf pro, you know."

"Mom! Timmy O'Donnell and his plaid pants! You've got to be kidding. I'd be doomed to a life of Long Island Iced Teas in the club while he hardy-har-hars with a bunch of guys with cigars."

"Could be worse," my mother said.

No, it couldn't, I thought.

///

Terminator played on the overhead monitors as our bus roared toward San Miguel. "Look, Mom," I said, pointing out the window at a roadside Virgin of Guadalupe shrine. "You see these all along the highway." I didn't tell her that the crosses dotting the side of the highway were grave markers.

We came upon a formation of people walking, carrying fringed Virgin of Guadalupe banners. Their sweaters were draped over their heads in the midday heat, knit arms swaying.

"Mom, a pilgrimage! My Spanish teacher from the summer said pilgrimages give some people a chance to get away from the village, drink pulque, and be with a lover."

"Hrrumph."

"I run in the foothills in the morning," I told my mother. "Up the back of a mountain. At the very top is a large cross in a cement base. Every day there are fresh flowers in a coffee can at the base. There are no houses in the area. Somebody makes a long daily walk to leave flowers at the cross."

"I guess not too many people here have cars."

So much for hoping for an appreciative sigh from my mother. I wanted her to love the humble peasant and his religious devotion, to recognize the beauty of the lone mesquite tree we passed, casting a patch of shade on a parched field.

"It's so dry," she said. "Look at how brown everything is."

In San Miguel, we walked the cobblestone streets. In a hat shop, my mother plunked a straw sombrero on my head. Further up the street, she bought me shoes.

"Look at how the women carry their babies in *rebozos*,

close to the body. Isn't it beautiful?" I said, turning toward the Jardín. A moon-faced baby peeked from his mother's tightly wrapped shawl. The mother carried plastic bags in both hands.

"That baby looks hungry," my mother said.

We toured the Parroquia, where robed and bewigged statues stared back at us.

"See those *milagros*, Mom?" I pointed to little metal eyes, legs, heads pinned to the saints' clothes. "People leave those as thanks when they are cured."

My mother fingered a tiny heart. "How about the miracle of finding antibacterial soap in a store here?"

"Mom," I sighed.

"*You* go native then. I like hot showers and Half and Half in my coffee. Speaking of coffee, can we get one?"

"Nescafe with hot water in metal pots is it, Ma. Let's try a cool drink. Come on." On the west side of the Jardín, I bought us milky rice drinks called *horchata*. We sat on a bench. It was just after five. The sun was beginning to make long shadows of the Parroquia spires.

"Tastes like ice cream," my mother admitted, sipping.

A Bimbo bread delivery truck pulled up.

"Bimbo!" my mother laughed. "Go sit on the wall in front of the truck. Susan in Mexico. This will be something to show your father." She snapped a picture.

Hey ma, want to really see a bimbo, I thought about saying as I smiled at the camera. I can't get my mind off a nineteen-year-old.

Three days later, I waved down a green taxi outside El Instituto's doors and tossed my mother's bag into the trunk when the driver popped it open.

"Don't they help you with your bags here?" my mother said, in a last attempt to show me that the only way to the good life was to flee Mexico and its primitive ways.

The near-deserted bus lobby was lit by blinking Christmas lights around the Virgen de Guadalupe shrine. The waiting motor coach chugged in the back lot. Celaya, Salamanca, Irapuato and smaller destinations were inked on neighboring bus windows in white shoe polish.

"You'll come home in December, right?" my mother asked, turning before boarding.

"Yeah," I said, shrugging. "Let me finish the semester."

Satisfied, she climbed onto the bus. Realistically, I couldn't stay in Mexico forever. I turned and left the bus station. I jogged to my apartment in a papaya-hued dawn.

KISS

It was the last weekend in September and classes were cancelled for the feast of San Miguel, a fiesta that began at dawn with a deafening firecracker battle in front of the Parroquia, enacting the confrontation between St. Michael the Archangel and the Devil.

"Teacher, we're having a party tonight. Come!" the students implored on Wednesday before the long weekend. They wrote the address on a piece of notebook paper.

Nightfall, I put on a short swingy skirt and my cowboy boots. An evening stroll, I told myself. There was the house, not far from where I lived, the patio strung with paper lanterns. Mexican rock music blared, and my students milled about with long-necked Coronas in hand.

"Teacher!" someone yelled. "Teacher's here!" A girl in a jeans jacket grabbed me by the wrist. "No, no, I'm not staying. I was just out for a walk," I protested, as I passed through the gate.

Carlos was by the grill, holding a paper cup and talking to a taller guy who looked like him. His eyebrows shot up when he saw me.

I watched him come toward me. He walked like my brother. An athlete's walk.

"Rum and Coke?" I asked, pointing to his cup.

"Coca. Want one?"

"Sure."

He reached into a cooler.

"Teacher, come dance," said one of my second hour students, a curly-haired boy with a wispy mustache. Carlos returned then, handed me my Coke and glared, and the boy slunk away.

The look-alike came over. He was a tall Ray Liotta type—smoldering good looks and pockmarked cheeks.

"This is Hugo, my brother," Carlos said. Hugo wore a Guatemalan cap. It would have looked ridiculous on half the boys in the moonlit yard, but on Hugo it looked stylish.

"How old is he?" I said out of the side of my mouth.

"Seventeen," Carlos said. "He's in your 3 o'clock class."

"I know." My mother should see this, I thought.

"*Oye, guey*," Carlos' brother said. I heard *parque, rebote, basquet*. Basketball, I thought. They're talking basketball.

"Hey," Carlos said a few minutes later, and with a head jerk, led me away from the crowd, to the shadow of a eucalyptus tree. From under the leafy branches, we watched students drinking Coronas.

All my life, I'd wanted a man like my father – kind, strong, doubtlessly sure of the inner rudder that set his path. Few had lived up. What compelled me to follow a nineteen-year old with his dumb cholo haircut into the dark shade?

"There's going to be an earthquake in late winter," Carlos said.

Is that how boys impressed girls here, predicting natural disasters? "How do you know?" I asked.

"You'll see." By the brick grill, a kid in Carlos' class was arguing loudly about a soccer team. "Rodolfo always talks too loud," Carlos said, following my gaze. "He doesn't know who his mother is, and, well, nobody teases him anymore, but he's always afraid someone will."

"How…?"

"His mother was the maid. His father is a rich doctor. He got rid of her when Rodolfo was born and kept the baby. So Rodolfo comes to school on a motorcycle, in the best clothes, but…"

"But he doesn't know who he is."

Carlos' look told me he was pleased I got it. I liked his sureness. I stayed where I was, and watched him take a step closer to me. Then I breathed slowly and willed him not to move away.

"Let's go to the Jardín," Carlos suggested around 1:00 A.M. We stood by the beer tubs. Carlos had suggested we rejoin the crowd earlier when he saw Hugo wandering around aimlessly. "The fireworks will start soon."

Then I was walking down the Ancha de San Antonio with two good-looking almost-men, not wanting to be anywhere else in the entire world. Carlos smiled at me when his brother wasn't looking. At the door to El Instituto, I stopped.

"I'm very tired. I live here," I told Carlos. I had moved out of my summer casita with the goatskin rugs and now occupied a less expensive teachers' apartment in the college. "I'm going in." I stepped up, turned around, and gave him a quick Latin kiss on the cheek. Everybody does it, I told myself. My heart beat rapidly. I fumbled with my keys. Carlos' cheek remained close to mine. "I like your kiss," he whispered.

When I turned, he was walking away, saying something to Hugo.

In bed, I read for half an hour, comprehending little, until my heart calmed down and I could sleep.

///

The next afternoon, Carlos waited after class again. "Come with me to Laberintos this Sunday."

"All right," I said, lowering my voice and looking over my shoulder. "I will."

Listen, I can't make it, I'm sure by Sunday night I'm going to have typhoid; I rehearsed in my head the next day. Carlos watched me write *esperar*—to wait, to hope—on the board. I thought of the school director, how he would tuck his tie into his pants when he berated me.

///

Sunday at nine, I pulled on my motorcycle boots. I dressed in black jeans and my sleeveless powder blue velvet fifties top. Make-up or no make-up? I asked the mirror. I twirled on mascara and colored my lips pale pink.

I pushed open El Instituto's door fifteen minutes early to wait for Gussie, whom I'd invited so I wouldn't be on a real date, and found Carlos, leaning against the doorway, in white jeans, a paisley shirt and black boots. Mexican men were always late, an American girl had said at a summer party. And they always go out on their women. But here he was, not late at all. Carlos greeted me with a nod.

"We have to wait for Gussie, a friend."

"*Bueno.*"

We stood on the steps together. I watched the night wind blow through his hair. I was going to a disco, to stand close to him covered by darkness and music, not just watch him from yards away. Small talk died on my lips.

Gussie walked up the Ancha in a Mao Tse Tung T-shirt just as Hugo turned onto the street from Calle Orizaba and the four of us fell into step. The hamburger man was setting up his stand on the street. A naked bulb dangled over a stack of onions, towers of sliced tomatoes, red and yellow plastic bottles. Carlos walked on the outside. He's being gentlemanly, I thought with surprise. I tried to imagine a date in Philadelphia protecting me from traffic and could only think of some faceless boy next to me on Spruce Street, walking hunched against the cold, hands in his jacket pockets, until we reached Dirty Hank's, which wasn't called dirty for nothing, where he would stride in the door in front of me and order two seventy-five cent tap beers without asking me if I wanted one.

I drifted over to the curb to test Carlos. I hid my smile when he stepped down into the street and herded me back.

Thumping bass greeted us at the doorway of Laberintos. Labyrinths. What maze was I getting myself into?

Nobody in the disco looked older than fourteen. Girls wore short shiny dresses, heels and long bangs that curled on the forehead in an enormous half-loop. When I was in high school, girls had rolled their hair around orange juice cans to get the same effect.

We sat on some carpeted steps. Couples were glued together in corners. One pair was entwined above us, the girl's patent leather high heeled foot tapping.

Gussie jumped up. "Let's dance!"

The wooden floor was almost empty.

"I want more people out here so we can mosh!" Gussie yelled over the music. She danced like she was in Revival at 3 A.M., eyes closed, arms swinging around her head. I stomped my boots. Carlos moved across from me, his face a mask, until I caught his eye and he smiled quickly.

"I'll get this round," I said when we sat. "Coronas!" Gussie and I told the waiter. Hugo and Carlos asked for Coca Colas.

"Make mine a Coke," I said. "Una Coca."

Shifting around to accept our drinks when the waiter returned, Carlos's leg pressed into mine. Neither of us moved away.

I couldn't look at him, the thrill was so great. I sat, enveloped by thundering music, hardly breathing, feeling the warmth of Carlos' thigh.

Gussie pulled Hugo onto the dance floor. Carlos and I sat on the carpet, pressing our legs together. I noticed a handsome *café con leche* colored young man, dressed in American jeans. He saw Carlos and came our way.

"*Guey*," Mr. Cool and Handsome greeted Carlos. Guey—the Mexican version of dude.

"Memo," Carlos returned. "*El es Memo*," he told me.

"*Te presento a Susana*," he told Memo. Carlos had never called me anything other than Maestra before. My name on his lips had an exciting intimacy.

Memo eyed our legs mashed together. "*Rayando el sol, oh-wee-oh*," a group called Maná sang over the speakers. Carlos and Memo began to sing. Memo spread his hands and mouthed the words to me. He turned to Carlos, cocked his head and crooned to him. Carlos sang back.

Carlos turned to me then, and Memo dropped to one knee. "*Es mas facil llegar al sol que a tu corazon*," they sang to me. It's easier to reach the sun than your heart.

The lights went down and the music slowed. Carlos put his hand on my back and we stepped onto the dance floor. Carlos held my right hand and encircled my waist like a ballroom dancer, and we moved with small steps. Another slow one, I prayed when the song ended. It was, and Carlos dropped my hand and put his arm around my neck.

My cheek was precariously close to Carlos' face. I took discreet gulps of air to drink him in. Then his cheek touched mine. It was completely smooth, like no man's cheek I'd ever felt before. It was like a baby's skin, like butter, like air after a rain. We moved in a circle, touching at the waist, the shoulder, the cheek. The world was pure sensation—music, glittery light from the sequined ball above and Carlos' skin. Then our cheeks slid until our lips touched. We kissed, slowly, slowly, suspending the moment into one long taffy pull of time. *Just a girl kissing a boy.* In that moment, I did not feel my future shifting, my destiny revealing itself. I felt only the meditative state I'd pursued, the world reduced to consciousness, in which all else drops away.

FAMILIA

Monday, I locked my apartment door and walked to class filled with excitement and dread. What happened in Mexico to someone who had kissed a student? I would be handcuffed, jailed, made to appear before parents for stoning. I could try denial. But there had been another El Pipila student at Laberintos, a kid who'd entered the dance contest and done a moonwalk. Maybe we had been too high up on the carpeted steps for him to see us. Then again, maybe he did see us dancing. Maybe now was the time to run to the Central de Autobuses and hop on the first bus going north.

Carlos sat in the front row in long satiny shorts and sneakers. I tried to look at the whole class and not just at him. But it was like he was made of neon or had an aura around him like the Jesus painting our next-door neighbors had when I was a kid. In fact, he reminded me of our neighbor, Joey Peters, only with a darker complexion. Joey was forever playing basketball in the driveway between our houses. The sound of dribbling and a ball hitting a rim was the background music of my childhood. And almost all the scenes of my early life had a ball and a hoop in them—Joey Peters in Converse high tops; boys doing passing drills at my dad's Pocono Mountain basketball camp, Sunday night games at Aronomink Swim Club, visiting my dad during practice at the St. Joe Fieldhouse. I had not seen many men wearing shorts in Mexico, but Carlos seemed comfortable in them.

Carlos gave me a quick raise of the eyebrows when I allowed myself to look at him. I touched the black cross I hadn't taken off since the day he put it over my head, then quickly turned to the board.

To make, to do, I wrote. I was teaching action verbs. *To ask, to wait, to dance, to kiss.*

"How do you say *hacer el amor*?" asked a skinny kid who, when we had done names, had flexed a muscle and told me they called him Marky Mark Mexican.

"Hacer is translated as to make or to do," I said. I liked to get the students to figure things out. "And you all know how to translate amor. O.K., write a sentence using one of the verbs we've just learned."

Heads bent over papers, then craned back and forth.

At four o'clock, the students dropped their assignments on my desk, and filed out the classroom door. I leafed through the papers. Every single student had written the same thing: "Do you want to do the love?"

Carlos' handwriting was small and neat. I looked around furtively. Carlos was standing in the hall, outside the door, smiling his little smile at me.

I plopped my books down on the bed in my bathtub-sized apartment and looked at myself in the mirror. You are a 33-year woman who, only months ago, gave up chasing busboys so you could grow up, I scolded. Outside, voices of the painting students who had just finished an afternoon class drifted through my door. "Roger never draws eyes. Did you notice?"

"There's something weird going on there." The voices diminished, as the students walked under the high stone arch outside my apartment and rounded the corner.

I took my running shoes from under my bed, slipped them on and yanked at the laces. As I stood, I heard, coming under the arch, a basketball bounce, then another, the sound ringing off the flagstones. I stuffed my head bandana back into the drawer and went to the window, hiding behind the curtain to peek out.

Carlos wore the same basketball shorts from class but next to him, Hugo had him beat with an even more oversized pair of bright blue satin bottoms. The boys had stopped outside the classroom across from my apartment. Hugo spun the ball on his index finger while they conversed in Spanish.

I kept the curtain around me for thirty seconds, holding my breath. Then I grabbed a blank envelope and walked outside with it, clearly on my way to the Instituto office with a letter to mail.

"Oh, hi," I said, raising my eyebrows in surprise. Hugo bounced the basketball like it was his language. Bounce—time to go. Carlos jerked his head toward the entrance. I was supposed to just follow them? I crossed my arms. At the arch, Carlos turned around. I examined my fingernails. He came back then, and waited while I put my "letter" back in the house.

Juarez Park was several lush acres of low, fat-leafed vegetation and high pecan and ash trees shading packed-dirt walking paths, anchored by full-length basketball courts.

"Do you play basketball?" I asked as Carlos and I entered the park, passing a circular area where boys were practicing bull fighting with shopping cart bulls.

"We play on the Ring team on Thursday nights," Carlos said, glancing at his brother. An athlete—I knew it! Something in common.

So Thursday nights Carlos was here in the park. Sundays in Laberintos. Where did he spend the other nights of the week? I tried to picture Carlos in some house at night, doing his homework, but figured that wasn't quite right. He and Hugo never carried many books to or from school. What I thought of was my childhood house on Anderson Avenue and the velvet couch my mother had liberated from the curb one large-item trash day and on which I used to lay and read Nancy Drew mysteries. I pictured my dad on the upholstered chair next to it, reading the paper. Did Carlos have a favorite chair, a favorite book?

In the park, small Mexican men in nylon uniforms and everyday tennis shoes ran up and down the basketball court, some of them out of shape and puffing.

"That one," Carlos told me indicating a wiry player in odd low cut sneakers that resembled ballet shoes. "They call him Pollo."

"Why do they call him Chicken?"

"Look how skinny his legs are."

Pollo was a human energy molecule, moving from under-the-basket to under-the-basket, the full length of the court, while the other players were still thinking about it. He made lunging steal attempts, launched himself into the air for rebounds and dived for loose balls with a great show of flying elbows. Pollo's teammate rebounded a missed shot and threw him a quick pass. Pollo took off at breakneck speed.

"Go!" I cried. Pollo missed. The other team rebounded and ran down court. The short guy Pollo was guarding caught a pass then took several steps into the lane with the ball clutched at his chest.

"He walked!" I screamed. I turned to Carlos. "Did you see that?" Carlos watched the game with a stony face.

"Didn't you see that walk?" I repeated.

"*No grites*. You don't yell here," Carlos told me.

I looked around. Two teenage girls in the stands twirled their hair. The rest of the spectators could have been watching a chess tournament. I crossed my arms, kicked a tree root.

"I think *I* know how to watch a basketball game," I said.

"It's not a good idea to call attention to yourself."

"That's not how it is where I come from," I said testily. Should I just leave, or say adios first?

"I've wondered how hard it is to live outside your country," Carlos said.

'You have no idea,' I said drily. It's not the don't-drink-the-water, don't-wear-pants issues. It's that you're an American and guys are looking at you and you haven't developed the icy manner of a Mexican *fresa,* a shielded rich girl, to hold them off yet. And you're outraged when Mexican men expect you to go to bed with them because you're American, but you have to tone down your righteousness because in the case of some, like the vacation girls, it's true. Like at a small party I'd had that previous summer, where, at around one A.M., two Mexican guys I didn't know and who I soon kicked out, began arguing over who was going to get to spend the night with me. As if I was invisible! As if I had no say in the matter! In my own house!

"I grew up watching hoops," I said, and then stopped. I barely knew this kid. I was acting like an escapee from a high school sitcom. "I've got to go," I said.

"I'll walk you home," Carlos said, and fell into step beside me.

We didn't say much on the walk back to El Instituto. I realized it felt alright.

My life was getting sidetracked. I hadn't thought about what to do with my future in days. This affair (non-affair) needed space, before things got out of hand. In class the next day, I nodded curtly and swept my gaze over Carlos' head.

After class, I returned to my apartment and dumped my books on my little table, exhausted from being emotionally distant from Carlos. My stomach rumbled, and as I crossed my room to check the refrigerator I saw him through the window, leaning against the stone classroom wall. I turned, heart pounding. Guys in Philly were cagey and unavailable. This guy was decent, pursuant.

I pretended I hadn't seen him and continued to the kitchen. I hid there for two full minutes. Then I grabbed my sweatshirt.

Carlos steered us to the park but we passed the basketball courts and walked up past the Chorro, the old city waterworks, as the sun set. "We used to come here and bathe in the holding tanks," Carlos said. "Before we had water in our house."

"No water?" I said.

"And my sisters brought the wash here," he pointed at the Lavanderia, a row of some ten outdoor sinks where aproned women scrubbed clothes in the flowing water.

"My sister, Patricia, used to get in fights. Nobody was going to take *her* space. She'd clock any señora who even *looked* at her soap."

One of my eyebrows shot up. The señoras at the wash sinks didn't exactly look like society women. I reduced the size of the house I imagined Carlos in.

"What did you do while your sisters were washing clothes?"

"Went to the park," Carlos shrugged.

"We used to play Kick the Can and Capture the Flag when I was a kid," I said after a pause. "And swam at Aronomink Swim Club. And played tennis." Did I sound hoity-toity?

I followed Carlos up narrow cobblestone streets built for burro traffic, through a part of the city I did not know, emerging in a wider street where a few cars chortled lazily up the incline. "They call this El Mirador," Carlos said when we stopped at a lookout. The sky had darkened and the city twinkled below us. The spires of the Parroquia were outlined with lights.

"I've never been up this high. What a sight!" I exclaimed. Carlos was standing very close behind me. I leaned into him, and suddenly became shy – wasn't he mad that I'd ignored him in school?

His arms encircled my waist.

"This reminds me of how we slept as kids," he said.

"Now what are you talking about?"

"We all slept together like this in one bed, all my brothers and sisters."

"On cold nights?"

Carlos laughed. "All the time."

"Ummm." I groped for something to say. "How many of you are there?"

"Six."

"You slept six in a bed?"

"Sí. We didn't have a door, only a curtain so we told scary stories about what was going to come in and get us."

"No door."

"Worse than the bogey man were the rabid dogs. We could hear them."

"I slept in the top of a bunk bed with my sister," I said, then stopped. How could I match his stories? I'd walked to school with my sister and brothers. My mother had read us stories and kissed our foreheads goodnight – a Brady Bunch childhood, only no maid.

We watched the city.

"Where were your parents?" I asked.

"My mother slept in the bed next to us. My father was

in Mexico City, working."

"What kind of work?"

"Building. My mother and father almost didn't have us," Carlos said. "My mother was seventeen, working in a *molina*, where they grind the corn for tortillas. My father had been coming around, taking her to the movies, taking her anywhere she wanted to go, she says, never leaving her alone. Then one day she was leaning in the doorway of the molina, talking to another girl who worked there, and the girl suddenly pulled her violently by her apron. My mother turned around and saw a wild-eyed woman lunging at her with a knife.

'Stay away from my man!' the woman shrieked. 'He's mine. We're married. I have his son. Don't go near him!' She jabbed the knife at my mother."

"My mother did a quick sidestep, picked up a Coke bottle and cracked it in half on the window ledge," Carlos continued. "She knocked the knife out of the woman's hand and cut her with the bottle. There was blood all over her face. They took the woman to the hospital and kept her there for two days. The police came looking for my mother but she had gotten on a bus to Celaya. She stayed with a cousin who found her a job. She planned to never see my father again."

Carlos had never spoken this much before. I didn't want to interrupt, especially since I had to concentrate so hard to understand his Spanish.

"They threw my father in jail, so he would tell them where my mother was. But he didn't know. Then he got out after a couple of days and went to see my mother's brother. My uncle told him where my mother had gone; so then my father went to Celaya and found her.

'That woman left me,' he told her. 'Yes, we have a son, but I haven't been with her in years. She has children by other men. She's got no hold on me.'

My mother gave in and they went to Queretaro to live. We were all born in Queretaro."

"Wow," I uttered like an American mall kid. Romance, passion, violence! How could I top that? "My dad was a basketball coach," I said.

"Really?" Carlos turned toward me. That statement always got a reaction. A high school coach—people usually asked. College? Carlos waited.

"He coached in the NBA," I said.

Sometimes, given this information, a person would recite my father's coaching history back to me. "Jack McKinney, yeah! He coached the Lakers and had that accident. Fell off a motorcycle, didn't he? Or a bicycle? The Lakers won the championship that year and your dad went on to Indiana. Hey, wait. He was with the Portland Trailblazers too, wasn't he? He coached Bill Walton, Kareem Abdul Jabbar and Magic Johnson. He's got a championship ring, doesn't he?"

"Two," I'd say.

"I love basketball," Carlos said. "I've seen a few games in El Sexy's house. He has cable television. You actually went to NBA games?"

"A million of them."

"So that's where you learned to yell at games." He was grinning now. "What was that like for you?"

"Yelling?"

"Growing up in an athletic household?"

Usually I was told I ought to write a book about my dad. Or, about the history of St. Joe's College basketball. What was it like for *me*?

"Well, my father wore shorts to work for one thing. He'd get out of the car at the end of the day still wearing his whistle, and when I was young, I wished he was like Mr. O'Neill next door who wore an overcoat and a hat and came home at 5:30 on the dot and never worked on

Saturday," I said in English. Carlos nodded his head. "After awhile I realized the neighborhood boys never tried to throw their football to Mr. O'Neill. And that Mr. O'Neill never got his name in the newspaper."

"Is he still coaching?"

"Retired. Selling sporting goods for a Philly company. Your dad?"

"He lives with us now. He worked in Mexico City for about fifteen years, but now he's in San Miguel."

Carlos and I watched the stars for a while. Walking back to the center of town felt like walking back down to earth. We made out like teenagers in El Instituto's darkened doorway. The *velador*, the night watchman prowled by, inspecting us. One night I'd seen him sitting on a patio bench, cleaning his pistol.

"*Buenas noches,*" Carlos said.

"Buenas noches," I sighed. I guessed it wouldn't do to have a teacher invite the student inside after dark. When I passed the velador on the way to my apartment, he patted the bulge in his jacket pocket.

PROMENADE

"Let's go to the Ring. I've never been there," I suggested a few nights later. Carlos had gotten into the habit of coming by the Instituto after dark and standing on the steps outside, as the big street doors were locked at seven. Then I came out, and usually we walked to the Jardín and sat on a bench.

El Ring discotheque had a boxing theme. The dance floor was the ring, the seats were tiered around it. We settled ourselves at a lower table and ordered a beer for me and a Coke for Carlos. I excused myself to go to the bathroom. Walking back to our table, a young man with thick caterpillar eyebrows placed himself in front of me.

"*Quieres bailar?*"

"Hm?" I said. "Oh, all right." I was following him toward the dance floor when my arm was grabbed.

"You're with me," Carlos said firmly.

"Oh!" I said, startled again. I followed him back to the table, my hand in his. In Philly the worst thing you could be was *clingy*. If I went to a club with a guy, I always danced with others to show I was not. I talked to everyone at parties. Nobody would call *me* possessive. Here, the rules confused me. But I liked being claimed.

"Guey!" It was the handsome chilango who, with Carlos, had sung to me in Laberintos, calling from the dance floor. Carlos gave an upward nod in greeting. Memo jumped down from the dance floor and deposited his drink on our table. A swingy ranchero tune started up. "*Me das permiso?*" Memo asked Carlos.

"*Sí,*" Carlos replied, giving his friend permission to dance with me. Memo took my hand. I looked inquiringly over my shoulder and Carlos nodded. Memo swung me around. I had lived in Wisconsin and danced the polka at weddings. I one-two-threed enthusiastically, smiling at Carlos, who sat alone at our table as we whizzed by. Then the music slowed and Memo pulled me closer to him, his hands roaming my back. Memo steered us into the far corner. The lighting was dim. When Memo bent me backwards, I felt the top of his leg nestle for a long beat between mine. "*Quieres salir conmigo?*" he asked, lifting me to a stand-and-shuffle position again.

"What?" I said loudly over the music. I couldn't have heard right.

"Do you want to go out with me?" Memo repeated, his hands moving lower and lower on my back.

"No, I'm going out with your friend," I said, shifting around to hitch his hands away from my buttocks. We were swaying in place now. Memo kept his back to our table. I could not see Carlos.

"You can go out with me, too." I thought of what Gina had said at a party—"Mexican men think we're all dying to hit the sack with one of them and it takes no work to get us there. Plus they're all married, whether they tell you so or not."

Memo's arms crisscrossed my shoulder blades. I glimpsed my boyfriend, sitting alone while his friend hit on me. I shook myself free and hurried back to Carlos. I felt like I had rancid oil on my skin.

"I got to know Memo when he moved from D. F. Besides family, I was the only one at his wedding," Carlos said. "Just a small party in his parents' house next to the carpentry shop."

"He's married?" I tried to keep the surprise out of my voice.

"Sí."

"But he's always out alone."

"Sí."

"Doesn't his wife ever go out with him?"

"She stays home with the baby."

Couples twisted and sweated on the dance floor. In the opposite corner, Memo eyed the unattached women.

My teacher friend, Barb, had told me about a girl who went out with a Mexican guy they called El Raton. She didn't understand that that was like calling him Thief. He moved into her house, and months later moved out again, taking her money, jewelry and furniture. He'd even taken her prized baseball mitt signed by some famous player.

I twisted to look into Carlos' eyes to see if he was trustworthy, but the room pulsed with disco lights, and his long lashes, his gentle mouth only lit up in glimpses.

I paced my apartment the next night. I could go to grad school at Temple and study writing, I thought. It was an unusually cloudy dusk. I considered going out to the wind-swept patio to brood but figured there was no use being dramatic if there was nobody to witness it. Writing my memoir about being the coach's daughter in an MFA program had been my plan before I left Philly. It seemed like just the thing to set my sights on now, before I got in too deep with the teenager who kept occupying my thoughts.

The clock ticked toward seven-thirty. Carlos was surely outside on the Instituto steps, like he'd been every night for the past two weeks. I picked up a little devil on a motorcycle, one of the ceramic figures that adorned the apartment. He looked diabolically happy about riding into the unknown on his chopper. This is what I would do: get serious again about writing my book, finish the semester at the prepa, go to Philly, find a guy, have a baby. Throw a wedding in there first. Forget the nineteen-year-old out on the steps.

I exited my apartment. I should do something reckless, I thought, to throw off these horrific visions of having a middle-of-the-road life. I should rustle around unseen in some bushes, and make the *velador*, the night watchman, pull out his gun. Instead I went to the front of the building and opened the street door.

///

"Everybody get up out of your seats and form a circle," I said to my four o'clock class.

"Now, I start. I will give a command. The person to whom I give the command follows. Nacho, *go* to the door." Nacho watched me with concentration. "*Go* to the door." Nacho pointed to the door, understanding, and bounded to it.

"O.K. Come back." I motioned with my arm. "Now, your turn. You give a command."

"*Beatriz, que beses a Marcos.*"

"Nacho, look. Here's what you say. Beatriz, kiss Marcos."

"Beatriz, kiss Marcos."

The class erupted into hoots, hollers and applause as Beatriz crossed the room.

What have I started? I thought. Carlos sat in the back, his face a mask.

"You can refuse a command too," I said.

"*Juan Pablo, que bailes con Areceli,*" Beatriz said after she kissed Marcos full on the mouth.

"Beatriz, say 'Juan Pablo, dance with Areceli. See? That's another command.'"

After Juan Pablo waltzed Areceli a couple of steps he told Cristobal to kiss the teacher. "*Que le beses a la Teacher!*" he shouted, as the school director opened my classroom door.

"I'm teaching commands," I tried to say in Spanish, reddening. The class laughed. What I had said, was, I'm showing them how to be the boss.

The director looked around the room then backed out, shaking his head as if he'd just mistakenly entered the women's bathroom.

///

"Hey, see you at the opening!" shouted Claudia, my fellow model, from across the Ancha.

"Right," I said, waving. The art opening was making me jittery as a June bug. It was Ted's big opening, a solo show of his work. He'd been working to finish his paintings for months and I'd been modeling at his home every Saturday. One sweltering weekend, Claudia had come over as well and Ted had put us naked together on a lounge chair in opposite directions. He painted us in a blue green background minus the chair, so we looked like we were tailless mermaids swirling in the ocean. The largest painting in the collection however was just me against a fiery orange background, again without the patio chair. My pubic region was highlighted with green sequins.

It was November. Ted was busy putting finishing touches on paintings for a solo show. It should have been exciting for me too with my image on several canvases, but I was nervous. I had only vaguely mentioned modeling to

Carlos, and had skipped the part about taking my clothes off. Now if I invited Carlos to the opening, would he still think I was a nice American girl?

Thursday of that week, Carlos and I walked up the Ancha from the Jardín. Ted's show opened the next night. I blurted, "Want to come to an art opening with me tomorrow night?"

"Yeah, I guess so. Where?" Carlos asked.

"Here," I said, stopping at my door.

Carlos showed up on the Instituto steps the next night, looking more grown-up than usual in a brown leather jacket. Gringas in Oaxacan blouses and big silver jewelry walked past us, on their way to the Galería Pergola. I took Carlos' arm, heart banging, and we walked under the wide portal toward the gallery.

On the wall across from the gallery entrance was Ted's largest painting, the green sequined nude. In Ted' studio it had seemed obvious it was me, but seeing it framed and hung now, the figure looked more like a giant girl with flaming hair about to turn into a dragon. My eyes looked like my eyes, but my face was done in reds, yellows and oranges. Next to me Carlos was studying it.

"So, is that you?" Carlos asked.

My palms went clammy. "Yeah."

"Sí, that's how you sit," Carlos said. I told myself to keep breathing, but his eyes had shifted to the next painting, two boldly drawn blue and pink street dogs dancing. We moved to the next one, and then walked along side-by-side looking at paintings. We stopped behind a crowd in front of the mermaids.

"Lesbians," a lady in a beret said in a low voice to her friend.

"Definitely," the friend whispered back through scarlet lips.

I fought the urge to giggle. Carlos turned toward me

and raised an eyebrow.

Out on the patio, I fetched us two plastic cups of red wine. A middle aged woman from Atlanta who had drawn me in Ted's classes waved hello. I waved back. Carlos kept his hands in his jacket pockets but nodded here and there. "If I'd known it was that easy to get you to take your clothes off," he said, touching on the subject we had never talked about. I fake-punched him in the ribs. For a minute, I forgot I was with a high school kid.

The feeling didn't last. The next night, Sunday, as I walked to the Jardín, two kids on bicycles zoomed next to my ankles. The plaza was alive with high schoolers, families, *elote* and popcorn sellers. I looked around for someone I knew, somebody my age maybe.

Instead my sights found two teenage girls laughing under a streetlamp, faces upturned. One raised a shoulder. The other adjusted a hair tie and twisted a hip. I remembered flirting like that. The boy they flirted with had his back to me, saying something to make them go "Oh!" with rounded mouths.

It was Carlos.

My vintage jacket felt musty, my flat shoes, shabby. I faded into the shadow of the Parroquia.

The girl who wore a skirt had a slim waist. She rested her elbow on her friend's shoulder and cocked her head. The ponytailed one laughed and pushed Carlos' arm. They were sixteen or seventeen years old.

I wanted to leave.

Carlos turned, scanning the evening crowd.

Two minutes. I'd give him two minutes to find me. If he failed, I would go home.

Carlos turned, checked the Parroquia clock. Peered through the crowd. I took a step, put myself in the light.

Carlos' face lit up when he saw me. That smile.

"Who are your friends?" I asked when he came over.

"Some girls from my neighborhood," he said, hand on my back.

"Yeah, I had lots of male friends in Philadelphia," I said. I heard what a fool I sounded like.

"Come on," Carlos said.

When I reached for his hand, he said, "No," but then smiled.

"What do you mean?" Now I was suffering that choking, insecure feeling I hated.

"We're going to *pasear*."

"Wha..?"

"Promenade. It used to be formal. On Sunday nights, single girls would circle the Jardín going north, and the boys walk the other way, south. Everyone checks everyone else out."

"Who are you going to be checking out?"

"Ha!" Carlos laughed. We were at the entrance that faced the Parroquia. To our right, the elote (corn) seller slathered a cob-on-a-stick with mayonnaise and sprinkled it with red chile powder. Carlos pushed me toward Calle Correo, which housed the post office. When I twisted my head, he was walking toward Umaran, about to turn right and head for the Banamex.

I walked to the corner and turned left, following the square. All around me, teenagers pushed and jostled each other. Girls sucked on lollipops innocently and seductively at the same time. Friends walked with arms hooked. Boys walked with hands jammed in their pockets. Eyes darted to the opposite sex, teasing, inviting. Around the far corner came Carlos.

"Now what?" I asked when we passed. I only had time to see his amused smile. OK, I thought. I'll play. For now.

We passed again in front of the Presidencia – City Hall. "If you like me, you turn and walk with me," he said before he was gone.

I had a whole block to cover before I had to respond. I hadn't let a boy chase me in a dozen years. Since the Player and the Agent and my silence, I hadn't believed I was worth catching.

The Parroquia clock said 8:30 on its brightly lit face. Carlos was probably opposite me, passing the north portals, while I passed the south. I turned to walk in front of the Parroquia and looked through the crowd for him. "Don't chase boys," my mother always said. "You look a little too…"

I was tired of being desperate. Carlos approached. His face looked like he would never wish me harm. We were going to cross paths right in front of the Parrish church. There he was, clearly amused at pretending not to see me. I could reach out, take his hand, touch his sleeve. He passed. I kept walking.

By the time I got to the corner I wanted to cry. He was walking away. I'd never see him again. I was an idiot to be playing a game with a teenager. I would circle the Jardín and keep walking back to my tiny apartment. I would wake up and make a serious plan for my life.

A sob caught in my throat at what a fool I was, but then it turned into a hiccup because Carlos was at my side then, one arm wrapping around my shoulders, squeezing the breath out of me.

DATING MEXICAN MEN

I walked down the Ancha, balancing a towering wrapped load of laundry that blocked my view.

"Teacher, what's up?"

I shifted my laundry and saw one of my four o'clock students, carrying a guitar case. His name was José but since he had an American father, the kids called him Joe. In class, Joe ignored me, occupied as he was picking out imaginary chords on an air guitar.

"Where are you going with that?" I asked.

"I was trying out a new drummer. I had a great band but it fell apart a couple of months ago. I've been trying to get another one going. This kid's O.K. but he's no Stewart Copeland, know what I mean?"

"You're a Police fan?" I'd been one since 1978, when I'd rocked out with my sister at their Indianapolis concert. Jen and I had worn Jamie-Lee-Curtis-doing-aerobics-bandanas around our heads.

"Jimmy Page is my Jesus."

"Stairway to Heaven" was the theme song to my Soph Hop," I said dreamily, then snapped back to a street in Mexico and my student standing in front of me. "I've got to go grade some papers."

"I'm bored with English, Teacher. No offense. I just want to study music. Man, I wish I could just play guitar all day."

"Am I that pathetic, Joe?"

"No, your classes are fine. Listen, forget about your papers. Let's go get a beer."

"How old are you?" I asked. Beer with a student – another sin.

"Almost twenty," Joe said. Almost an adult, I thought. Maybe I could have almost-adult conversation. We crossed the street to a restaurant called Hoboes and sat under a sad clown painting.

"Listen, Teacher. *Es que,* sometimes you don't get what's going on," Joe said, after he ordered two Coronas. "For instance, you say, '*Es la regla.*' It's the rule, meaning a grammar rule. But you notice how the kids laugh? Regla also means a menstrual period."

"Oh," I said, shrinking in my seat.

"Es que... Mexicans are great fans of the double entendre. *Picar* means to be hot, or to burn from heat, like when you say Pica! about this salsa." He indicated the chile-flecked red sauce on the table. "Picar also means to prick or jab." He drove his forefinger lightly into my arm. "*Picante* also means..." Joe spread his hands.

I reddened. Picante was hot and sexy.

"*Chingar*, which Americans think means to fuck, means more like fuck over. *Coger* is how we say fuck, meaning, you know."

"So, do you have a nickname?" I asked, to change the subject.

"Yeah, but I'm not going to tell you what it is," Joe

said, squeezing a lime. "Let's go to Pancho's!" he cried suddenly. "I used to play in Pancho's, with the house band sometimes. Look, drop your laundry off and I'll take my instrument home and I'll pick you up in ten minutes."

"I need to stay home tonight."

"See you in ten."

I threw my laundry on my bed and flopped down next to it. Carlos would be by in less than an hour.

Then Joe was tapping on my window. How did he know where I lived? In Philly, the best times with Joy and my artist friends had always had a spontaneous start. What was the unexamined life anyway?

///

Sawdust covered Pancho and Lefty's wooden floor, and the waiters wore red neck bandanas. Entering Pancho's seemed to electrify Joe, whose bristly hair gave him a plugged in look to begin with. He looked around, drumming his thumb on his chest.

"Once when I was playing, I went into a solo and the owner told me to stick to the program. He wanted, you know, a lot of Celebrate good times, come on."

Bartenders lurked behind lined up shot glasses. Joe ordered two Coronas and we sat at a table, like the one I'd occupied with Carlos at the Ring. I looked around guiltily.

"Wanna?" Joe asked, indicating the wooden stage. We stepped up. Joe danced with a strange combination of jutting elbows.

Next to us, an old pot-bellied American hippie who they said would sell you fake residency papers undulated as if he were at Woodstock. He danced with an American lady who took up the whole dance floor with her swirling Frida Kahlo skirt. I danced around her skirt while Joe did some white-guy movements. Dancing always made me happy. I was glad I had come.

At 1:30 A.M. the music went down and the lights, up.

"Let's go to El Ring!" Joe said. He urged me on by my elbow, and caught in the night's velocity, I walked ahead of him.

"This is the routine," Joe said. "On Wednesdays, everybody from Pancho's goes to El Ring until it closes."

The cigarette and candy sellers had folded their porttable trays and moved from Pancho's to the street in front of El Ring.

"Those guys don't get rich selling Marlboros. They have pot, coke, anything you want," Joe whispered as we ducked through the Ring's dim entrance. A Caifanes song was playing. Joe strummed an air guitar.

At 3 A.M., Joe stopped playing in his invisible band long enough to hold his arm out. I took his hand and we danced formally like a couple at a charity ball. Over his shoulder, I tried to pick out couples that were going to go home together. Or to a car – where did they go? Joe, I noticed just before he kissed me, was rapturously staring into my face.

Thin lips pressed mine and a tongue darted around like a trapped mouse inside my mouth. Shocked, I worked my arms to my chest and pushed. The lights went up. Joe took a breath, encircled my waist and kissed me again. I grabbed some hair at the back of his head and pulled his face away from mine.

"Teacher," he breathed. He thought I was being playful. I could see it in his smirky look. He thought I would be a biter and hair-puller in bed. When I shrugged his arm off my shoulder, he grabbed my hand. I shook it free.

On the street, I waited a few blocks until we were away from the dispersing crowd.

"Joe," I began.

"Teacher," he cut in. "Susan. I really like you. You're,

you know, so cool. And like, you're old but you're good-looking."

"Joe, listen to me. I'm with somebody else. I'm seeing another guy. Nothing's going to be happening between us." I couldn't wait to close the Instituto's big wooden doors behind me.

Joe asked, "Who are you seeing?"

"A guy in your class. Carlos."

"Ortega." He mulled that over, then poked my arm. "So, I'm not too young for you!"

We walked down the middle of Hernandez Macias. The moon was a shaved thumbnail.

"I went out with an older woman once. It was, like, totally sexual. She was only here for the summer. She wanted to try all kinds of things she'd probably only read about. It was great having sex all the time, but, guey, she was crazy."

We turned onto Calle Codo, our footsteps ringing off the stone paving.

"Ortega is a nice guy," Joe said. "Not a loudmouth. Keeps to himself."

"He *is* a nice guy. Joe, I prefer the whole class doesn't know."

"Yeah, the class shouldn't know. I won't say anything." We headed up the Ancha de San Antonio. "Well, Teacher, you and Ortega."

I smiled. A boyish crush, then, mature acceptance of rejection.

At El Instituto, I withdrew my key from my pants pocket. "Good night, Joe. I had a good time."

"I still think you're cool, and I'll help you in class when you need it."

My papers lay unmarked on my table. My table clock read 4:15. Still, I couldn't sleep, thinking of Carlos, sitting on the outside steps; me not coming out, and him, trudging back down Orizaba to his house, alone.

///

After school the next day, Carlos paced my bathtub-length apartment. I dropped my school papers on the table and turned to face him.

"Carlos, last night I ran into Joe from your class. We talked. It was nice to chat in English, you know? He was explaining things about Spanish I didn't understand. We had a beer, then went dancing. We ended up at El Ring."

Carlos stood still.

"At the end of the night, Joe kissed me, Carlos. I told him to stop. I told him I'm with you."

Carlos picked up a ceramic red devil riding a motorcycle from a shelf and put it down. "If you want some bar stud and the night life, just tell me."

"That's not what I want. I told Joe I'm with you. He said, fine. He won't be chasing me. There's nothing to worry about."

"You can't do that around here. People are going to talk."

"Do what?" I said, irritably.

"Go out with me and go out with him."

"I didn't *go out* with him." In Philly, I'd seen movies with Mark the busboy, and gone to art openings with Tom the waiter. I'd checked out a tapas bar in North Philly with Luis, the Mexican bartender who told me to come to San Miguel. The guys were friends and going to some event with them with nothing further happening was normal.

"What time did you get home?"

"You're not my father!"

"What time?"

"Around four."

"You go to the Ring with the guy till four and you're surprised he tries something?" Carlos couldn't believe how stupid I was. I was a Vacation Girl.

"Am I going to find his shoes around here?"

"Cut it out. I told you nothing happened!"

"Sí? Well, Hugo saw you."

"So?"

"He said the lights went up and you were kissing Joe in the middle of the dance floor, for everyone to see."

"I told you. I made Joe stop."

"Hugo wants me to drop you. All my friends too."

"So now your brother tells you what to do?" And the teenage gang too? I felt like I was in a John Hughes movie. "Maybe I should drop *you*!"

Carlos stared at me. I felt sick to my stomach. "That's not what I meant."

Carlos looked around the room. He was probably wishing for a nice little Mexican girl whose father made her come home by ten o'clock.

"I really didn't mean that," I said. My voice sounded frightened.

"Come on," he said. "Let's take a walk."

At the park, the stands were packed. The last city league basketball game of the night was in the first half. Across the court, Hugo watched from the sidelines with a prepa friend they called El Sexy.

We took a place on the opposite side. Carlos followed the game intently, hands in his pockets. A curly-haired man in a nylon warm-up jacket hurried by us, looking me over.

"That guy coaches one of the teams," Carlos said, without taking his eyes off the game. "He told me to look out for you."

"Yeah?"

"He says American women will give you AIDS."

The game was finished. The opposing team members shook hands. Carlos and I walked toward the Ancha. "Carlos, I don't have AIDS. I had a test before I came here."

Carlos looked at me sideways. I wished the words were

back in my mouth. He wanted to ask more, and didn't want to. He wanted to have a girlfriend who'd never heard of an AIDS test, but he had me instead.

///

"I met a guy!" Gussie stage-whispered, grabbing my wrist. Gussie lived in a small apartment on Cuna de Allende. She made refrigerator magnets and picture frames with bright swirly designs and shipped them to a Texas distributor of Mexican *artesania*.

"Come here. You've got to see this." She pulled me into a new store on the Ancha. The sign said Egan's—American Specialties. Triumphantly, she grabbed a box of Wheat Thins.

I looked around for the one American specialty I couldn't find anywhere—tampons—but Egan's shelves only held Vlasic pickles, Pillsbury brownie mix, packages of Chex mix and pretzels, bottled cranberry juice. At the counter, Gussie paid the equivalent of four dollars and tucked the Wheat Thins under her arm. Four dollars would have bought me food for at least two days.

In her apartment, Gussie served me six Wheat Thins on a plastic plate. I searched for words to tell her about the teenagers turning on me without sounding ridiculous.

"His name's Ricardo," Gussie said, plunking onto a cushion on the straight-backed wooden couch. "He has long hair. He kept staring at me at Mama Mia's the other night. Finally he came over to talk to me. I mean, I sat there looking available for long enough."

"And?"

"He's a lawyer," Gussie breathed.

"A long-haired, tongue-tied lawyer."

"He's from Me-hee-co. He's coming by at seven tonight."

"I went to the Ring until four in the morning last week,

and Carlos and his friends are still mad at me," I said.

"You're still seeing that *teenager?*"

"How old's your *lawyer?*"

"Consider that your *teenager* was in, like, first grade when the B-52s played their first gig," Gussie said. "Ricardo's twenty-five."

"And you're in your thirties."

Gussie sighed. "What are we doing?"

"Beats me," I said.

///

At the park that night, Carlos and I walked right up to Hugo and stood next to him on the sidelines.

"Worthless refs don't know how to call a game," Hugo said in Spanish.

"Those blasted fat guys are too slow to play basketball," Carlos added.

Carlos squeezed my hand, again and again. In my house, I'd found a photo I'd taken by holding the camera at arm's length. It was an autumn afternoon. I'd stopped Carlos and Hugo on the path leading to the basketball courts. Our faces were framed with park foliage. The brothers were on the outside and I, wedged in between them. There was the problem.

Hugo glanced at me sideways. His face was neutral now, the disgusted-with-his-brother's-girlfriend features gone. I stood watching, as I'd done at basketball games since childhood, a player in my own absurd life.

THANKSGIVING

On Thanksgiving Day, I packed a bottle of wine into a plastic market bag and tin-foiled the pecan pie I'd purchased from a Texas woman who, when she went to Immigration for a permit for her bakery, was promised by the director she would get it quickly if she took her clothes off.

"Thanksgiving – ever hear of it?" I asked Carlos. He and Hugo were sitting on the Instituto steps as I headed out.

"Sort of," he said. The brothers fell into step with me.

Something was bugging me. I wanted to be thankful for a tender boyfriend who kept me warm at night. But Carlos and I routinely went to the park or to the Jardín, and then he went home. If he was ever in my apartment, he acted nervous. For two months, I'd thought it was sweet. But now I was out of patience and filled with longing. Maybe Carlos had another girlfriend. Who knew who he hung out with in his neighborhood. I didn't even know where he lived. I also wondered if there was something wrong with him or me, or, of course, like my friends thought, something wrong with the whole thing we had going on altogether.

Walking past Laberintos, a boy with the same flat cheekbones as Carlos raised his head in greeting. He was with Raúl, one of my students.

"*Vamos a una fiesta,*" Hugo explained, or urged. The two joined us.

"Is that your brother too?" I whispered to Carlos.

"Si, that's Gerónimo, the oldest."

"Hi, I'm Susana," I said, when I saw nobody was going to introduce me. I stuck out my hand. The older boy shook tentatively. Four teenage boys were following me down the street and I carried only a pie and a bottle of wine.

"I should get another bottle of wine," I fretted.

"Aw, come on," Carlos said. We crossed the bridge on Quebrada, passing Canal where the liquor store was. I didn't have money for more wine anyway.

"*Hola, hola! Como estan?*" Nancy said, opening the door. "Who do we have here?" she said, looking over the neighborhood gang, the rat pack of scruffy but handsome boys behind me. None of them shaved, which was common with indigenous-ancestry Mexican men until about age 25. None was over twenty years old, to be more precise. I was a former television news reporter, a "personality" to some, arriving at a Thanksgiving fete with four boys and one dessert. I handed Nancy, an art student, the pie.

In the kitchen, Peter Ho was making pineapple margaritas. He painted at El Instituto too. His favorite subjects were men, preferably nude. Amber, an etching student, swept an arm sideways and foam sloshed over the top of the glass in her hand. "Greetings! I'm Canadian but here to celebrate anyway. Any excuse. Cute boys," she said conspiratorially. Gerónimo and the brothers huddled near the kitchen door.

"Yo!" Nancy called from the living room. "Somebody help me!" She was trying to coax a fire out of some fireplace logs.

"I can do that. My family's from Maine," said Gussie. She rolled up some old pages of El Atención, the weekly English-language newspaper.

"Where's the lawyer?" I asked, kneeling.

"You wouldn't believe it," Gussie said, brushing ashes from her jeans. "We went out a few times. Next thing you know, he's practically living with me. One night, he came to my apartment, all ready to come in and take a shower and I told him I wanted to be alone. He got this shocked look on his face. I said, 'I just want the evening to myself.'"

I nodded. Flames suddenly licked the log pile.

"I told him, 'Look, this is how I live. I need some space.' He turned and left."

William Ho stopped behind us with a tray of margaritas. "Just what I need," Gussie said, taking a glass.

"What happened next?"

"He banged on my door at midnight," Gussie went on. "When he wouldn't stop knocking, I opened the door. He held up his hand, blood all over it, blood dripping down his wrist. It had a slash across the palm. He said, 'This is what I have to do if I can't be with you.'" She looked at me. "I think he's crazy. I'm afraid to go out of my house."

"He's not a lawyer, is he?"

"He lives with his mother in Day Effay."

"He doesn't even have a job, right?"

"I'm done with Mexican men," Gussie said miserably.

The boys had migrated to the couch, where they attacked their margaritas as if they were Seven Eleven Big Gulps.

Shrieks of laughter came from the kitchen, where the Americans were apparently trying to make gravy with a *frijol* masher. The brothers and Raul snickered behind their hands, then stopped when Peter Ho came by with the blender offering refills.

Nancy pulled a giant turkey out of the oven and laid it on a side table alongside mashed potatoes, green beans, zucchini, salsa, a sweet potato called *camote* and a pot of frijoles. My crew parked their drinks on the floor and hopped up for plates. I lined up behind them then sat down again by the fireplace. The boys returned to the couch. Carlos looked from the couch to the fireplace and finally came and sat by me.

"Where's your friend's Chilango?" Carlos asked in Spanish. "Did she get tired of paying for everything?"

"How did you know?"

He looked at me pityingly. "We call guys like that *vividores*."

"Freeloaders."

"You'll find one or two sniffing around every American woman."

"We call people who go to a potluck empty-handed mooches and losers," I said.

"I've called my brothers worse than that for years."

On the sofa, the brothers and Raul were passing a bottle of wine back and forth. In the hall, Amber and Peter Ho agreed Jeff was hot, but were arguing over who Jeff, a Houston photographer, was going to go for, him or her.

Next to the fireplace, Gussie muttered, "Dateless on Thanksgiving," into her wineglass. Nancy looked around her living room, littered with food-encrusted plates and intoxicated friends. "I need a drink," she declared. She turned over one empty bottle after another.

"How about pie?" I offered.

"There's no booze left! Where did it all go?" In the kitchen, Nancy pushed casserole dishes aside, then looked in the trash and pulled out an empty tequila bottle. "The teenagers drank it. Who invited the teenagers? It's time for the teenagers to leave!" She said 'teenagers' as if they were a disease.

I indicated the door to Carlos with my eyebrow. He said something to his brothers, and they stood in unison, snickering. I herded the group toward the door.

"*Adios!*" yelled Peter Ho and Amber, remembering there were some Mexicans around and they could practice the thirteen Spanish words they knew.

"*Que se bañen! Que se bañen!*" Gerónimo and Hugo and Raul shouted at the door, arm in arm and weaving.

"*Hasta luego,*" the Americans cried, backlit in the front door.

"*Que se bañen!*" Carlos' brothers said, then looked at each other and laughed, almost falling into a flowerbed.

"*Que te bañes, guey,*" Hugo said to Carlos on the street, and doubled over.

"What are they saying?" I asked Carlos.

"*Que te compres jabón,*" Hugo told Gerónimo, who laughed so hard he had to support himself with his hands on his knees.

"They're saying," Carlos giggled, looking at his brothers. "They're saying, 'We hope you bathe'."

I didn't know who I was mad at: Gerónimo and Raul for drinking all the booze and being ungracious, or my American friends for drinking all the booze and being ungracious. Or at Carlos; I hadn't felt like part of a couple all night. He reached for my hand on the moonlit path; I pulled it away.

Wasn't going out with a bunch of teenagers a bit much already? Wasn't it time to hop a bus going north?

"*Que te tallas el trasero!*" Raul shouted into the night. Carlos laughed out loud.

Even though I gave him my I'm-getting-kind-of-pissed-here look, he didn't stop.

LOVE LETTERS IN THE SAND

"Be good," I said to Carlos.

"That's what I was going to tell you."

"I will. Don't look at me like that."

I kissed Carlos behind some plants on El Instituto's patio. It was December 18th, and the semester was over. Outside, forty kids were loading bags onto a bus that would take them to the beach for a Christmas vacation getaway, a trip sponsored by the high school.

"I'm going to miss you."

"Don't worry!" I said, looking at his worried eyes. "I won't even go out. I'm going to work on my book. I'll miss you too. Hey, you're getting an A in my class."

He unlocked his arms from around my shoulders and strolled out, as if he'd just been using El Instituto's bathroom. Out by the bus, Carlos talked to his brother, not to girls, I could see, spying from the patio. I watched them board, a bunch of eighteen and nineteen-year olds, heading away from their homes for five days, accompanied by teachers who looked barely older than them. Sand and sun, bikinis, and sneaked tequila—by nightfall, these kids were going to be in the mood to get friendly with one another. There was a particular girl who liked to sit next to Carlos in class, but I didn't see her anywhere. Still, my stomach churned.

At the Tuesday market, the ladies who offered herbs to cure your kidneys and lungs also sold little bags of powder to cure emotional ills. I'd paid five pesos for Legitimo Polvo de Contra Envidias. Anti-jealousy powder. 'Free yourself from envy and gossip, sprinkling this powder behind you as you leave your house,' the package read, I'd noticed as I'd trailed a line of the talcum across my doorway.

Blankets and boom boxes were tossed up onto the yellow charter bus, and with a squeal of air brakes, it pulled away.

Goodbye to jealousy of eighteen-year-old girls! Goodbye to hanging with teenagers! Goodbye to sexual longing! Good riddance! Who needed it? Carlos was either the most polite or the most hormone-deprived male I'd ever met. The thought of him with another girl – maybe that was why he had no hormones left over for me! This was torture. It was stupid. I had to go home.

My apartment had no phone so my parents couldn't reach me, and I'd avoided calling them. When Was I Coming Home for Christmas would be my mother's main theme, and I hadn't yet made plans.

Sometimes, like when Carlos was kissing me in the Instituto doorway, I thought I should see what Christmas in a foreign land was all about. I would buy a ceramic Mary and Joseph and some burros and cactuses and red devils from the Christmas market in San Juan de Dios, along with an oversized Jesus with his hands out like He was already giving blessings from His crib, or maybe like he was accepting wrapped presents. Get a little Christmas tree with its roots packed in a dirt ball. They sold firs about the size of my parents' neighbor's dog when he sat up to beg. The trees had no aroma and would never have inspired Andy Williams or Elvis to sing about them in a million years. By the end of Christmas week, I'd want to drink liquid Ajax.

I walked up the hill to the English school in a pair of rubber tire-soled huaraches, feeling the sun on my shoulders through my thin cotton shirt. The director paid me in cash on Fridays. I'd buy some supplies: tortillas, cucumber, tomatoes, chiles, beer. I'd make my last days in Mexico count. I'd write. And write. My book would take shape. By the end of the week, I'd be looking for an agent and informing my mother of my arrival.

Walking down the hill, my pockets jingling with pesos, I hummed, "Please don't go, don't go-oo," from the disco song Carlos and I had danced to. I shook my head. These were my five days to get the Mexican teenager out of my brain. He was too young for me! And besides we were too different. I grew up wearing white gloves to Mass, vacationing at the Jersey shore, watching Sunday dinners prepared in small linoleum kitchens by short, quick-tongued aunts who inhaled Lucky Strikes while they tied up the roast. He didn't have running water in his house until he was ten, skipped Sunday Mass to watch Lucha Libre on TV, and had never traveled beyond Querétaro, the next big town.

As I neared the bottom of the hill, Carlos and Hugo turned the corner and trotted toward me.

"Susana, get on the bus! There's one space left!"

"I have to…"

"Come on."

I looked from Carlos to Hugo and in that moment could not think of one reason not to follow them to the Pemex station where the bus was filling with gas. Carlos took my elbow and I let him lead me.

I climbed the bus stairs and stepped over knapsacks

until I reached the back seat of the bus and sat on the split upholstery between Carlos, Hugo, El Sexy and Raul.

The bus pulled onto the highway, rattling and chugging. Beyond San Miguel, ranchero children whacked the backsides of cows and squatted in curtained doorways of low makeshift houses with lamina—corrugated plastic—roofs. We passed a sign for Pantoja, a tiny village set back from the two-lane highway, and a panic gripped me. My return to my life as it was when I first came to Mexico—solitary, literary—a time away to clear my head of this foolish relationship—I had just denied it all.

A mile went by, then another. Hugo passed out tangerines. The boys spit their seeds out the windows with great teenage enthusiasm, their faces in the wind like happy dogs. Carlos's fingers played with the seam on my jeans, making me inert.

In the next state, the driver pulled into a dirt rest area lined with food shacks. El Sexy bought five hot paper bags of a fried snack called *fritura* and passed them around. I imagined hailing a truck, climbing in and getting off at the San Miguel crossroads. But Carlos put his hand on my shoulder, and I climbed back onto the bus.

Ahead of me, some forty kids screeched, hit each other, twisted in their seats, giggled, twirled their hair, and sucked lollipops. Several boom boxes blasted. What had I been thinking?

About midnight, duffels were opened and covers pulled out. "Don't you have a blanket?" I asked Carlos. He shrugged and opened his backpack for my inspection—gym shorts, T-shirts and a basketball. I slipped a New Kids on the Block T-shirt over my head and shivered in the cold night air. Under the cover of dark, I pressed myself close to Carlos and sniffed his clean skin. I'd read that newborns carried next to their mother experience cellular transference—something Mexican women who carried their babies in rebozos seemed to know. In the dark, I couldn't see the other kids on the bus. I imagined we were heading to a romantic beach vacation, *a solas*. I snuggled into Carlos' shoulder and he wrapped his arms around me.

The budget motel in Mazatlan was constructed of cinder block and metal. I asked the desk clerk if I could use the phone. The only person I knew in San Miguel who had a phone was a writer named Roy. But I didn't have his number. Phones were so hard to come by in San Miguel that an American couple I knew had set up a photo of a telephone in its intended spot, surrounded by flowers and candles—an altar to their phone-to-be. So I asked the clerk to dial my parent's number.

"Mom, hi! I'm at the beach. A school trip."

"Oh, you're chaperoning?" my mother asked from New Jersey.

"Uh-huh. It was a last minute thing. Just wanted to let you know where I am. See you in a week, Mom." I hung up before she could ask about Christmas. Images flooded my head though. Candles, spiced nuts, a cherry table that sat twelve, matching chairs with dusty rose velvet seats. The aroma of a tall Scotch pine filling the house, my father hugging a plaid bathrobe around him as he put on the Mario Lanzo Yuletide album we listened to every Christmas morning, singing Joy to the World elbow-to-elbow with my siblings at St. Joseph's church at the New Jersey shore.

In Mazatlan, we pulled into a parking lot constructed to hold large tour busses, and were shown to some second floor rooms with stunning parking lot views. Kids bunked four to a room and accommodations were spare. Even the motel I'd used when I crossed the border had provided soap.

My roommates were three girl students who acted as if I wasn't there. I leaned on the rail outside the room as the girls' belongings were already strewn across every inch of bed space and there was no place to sit. Carlos and his friends were assigned a room down the outdoor passageway. I was afraid to go down. First, if they were anything like my brothers, they'd be farting and telling really stupid jokes, and second, I figured I'd better be acting like one of the teachers. I didn't hold out much hope for bonding with the teachers, however. They were guys, and they looked about ten years younger than me.

I borrowed a swimsuit from a roommate called Araceli and ran down the stairs, across a busy boulevard and onto the beach. I splashed into the surf and dove into a wave. My cramped muscles began to tingle as they stretched. I surfaced and reached my arms toward the sun.

Carlos, Hugo and their friends crossed the sand in gym shorts and entered the water gingerly.

"Let's take a walk down the beach," I whispered to Carlos.

"Sure. In a minute," Carlos said, and ducked as El Sexy threw a piece of seaweed at his head.

"Look, Carlos. This is how we ride the waves at the shore where my parents live." I threw myself into a feeble wave that minced to the shore. At the Jersey shore on a good day, the waves were mighty, and if you caught one at the right spot in its curl, arms over your head, body straight like a surfboard, it would carry you in an exhilarating bed of turmoil and foam to within inches of dry sand. I loved being swept off my feet.

"Try it," I urged, standing.

Carlos looked dubious.

"You don't know how to swim, do you?" I asked. I dripped and squinted at him. "First thing to do is to get used to the water." I held out my hand.

"*Ven, guey,*" called El Sexy. Come on. Somebody had found a soccer ball and the boys were kicking it around.

Carlos stood knee-deep in salt water. He watched his

brother kick the ball. Then turned back to the horizon and took my hand.

///

A grizzled man with graying flyaway hair at the boat launch motioned to two small motorized dinghies with thick weathered hands. Our second day outing was a ride around the bay. The students began to step into the boats.

"Carlos, where are the life jackets?" I asked.

"It seems there aren't any," he said calmly.

"Carlos, I took Junior Lifesaving when I was a kid. If the boat goes over, don't try to make it to shore. I'll carry you in. You'll float and I'll pull you in like this." I hooked an arm under his armpit. "Or like this." From behind, I cupped my hand under his chin. We had been careful not to touch in the crowd, but this was survival. He shrugged out of my grip. "Let me carry you in. Don't try to swim. Promise?"

"Bueno."

He looked amused. We got in and the boats chugged out. I sat in the back with Carlos, Hugo, Raul, and El Sexy. In the next boat, my roommates were giggling, scooping up handfuls of water and tossing them onto a light-faced kid in a fisherman's hat. A girl in a tight T-shirt leaned into the shoulder of a light brown kid whose mother had delivered him to the bus in a sleek Dodge van, and a pudgy girl was listening raptly to the green-eyed physics teacher. White boys. The girls loved the light-skinned Mexicans, the fresas. I sat in back with the muscled brown boys, the guys who looked good in a sweat.

Everyone was flirting with someone.

"I'm going to fall over so you can save me," Carlos said. Raul pretended to push Carlos in, and Carlos grabbed me. "Not now," I hissed, but then he pulled me against him, and I sat in the boat with my ear on his chest, listening to his beating heart.

In the evening, students roamed from room to room. A few noisily played in the motel pool. My three roommates wore eye makeup that matched their short sets. A few dozen baby bottles of Corona beer had found their way into our shower stall, and boys were steadily showing up at the door. I wandered the outside halls. Carlos was taking a shower, Hugo said. Through the door, I saw El Sexy making a sandwich from some Bimbo white bread and tins of sardines and jalapeños.

"Sandwich, Teacher?" El Sexy asked.

"No, *ya comí,*" I answered, assuring him I'd already eaten although my stomach grumbled. One of the teachers lurched around the corner carrying a Coke that smelled like turpentine.

"Buenas noches!" he exclaimed, as if he'd just noticed I was among the group. "Do you give private English lessons?" He scrutinized me with slightly unfocused eyes.

"Why not?" I said. I could always use extra income.

"I want to take English lessons. Do you want a drink?"

I did. I wanted a drink. I wanted to go out for a nice seafood dinner. The teacher put his hand on my back and held his drink to my lips.

"We can arrange something for the week after vacation," I said.

"Why not now? In my room?"

"*Vamos.*" I heard it as a growl behind me. Carlos walked past me, his hair wet, his eyes hard. He went down the steps.

I took a quick gulp of the guy's rum and Coke, ducked out of his grip and ran down the steps.

I found Carlos at the corner, waiting for the traffic light to change. I caught up and we crossed the street to the beach. Carlos looked angry.

"What's the matter?" I asked. He shook his head. We walked down to the water. The strip of hotels faded into distant lights. The ocean drowned the highway sounds in the still night.

"Wait, I'm going to take my shoes off." He stopped and watched the horizon. I left my huaraches in the sand.

"Carlos, how do you say 'seaweed' in Spanish?" I asked as we walked. He was watching the sand in front of him now. He stopped and picked up a broken seashell. He wrote *algas* in the wet sand.

"How do you say 'sand', and 'seashell', and 'tide'?" I asked. He wrote *arena, concha* and *mareas*.

"Waves?" I asked.

He wrote *olas*.

"Upset?" I asked. "Angry?" He looked at me, and I felt what had intoxicated me from the beginning. Carlos *saw* me.

Carlos' hair had dried. It fluttered around a brown cheek. "That *payaso* doesn't want English lessons. He wants to *be* with you," Carlos said. "All the guys want to be with the gringa."

"What guys?"

"Not my friends. The teachers." All this time, and you still don't see through Mexican men, his tone said.

"Memo, my chilango friend, says on a scale of one to ten, if a guy can sleep with a gringa, it's a two, with a Chilean, it's a six, and with a Mexican fresa, it's an eight and a really good-looking fresa, a nine."

"Two?" I said indignantly.

Later, a Mexican co-worker would explain to me that Mexican men rented American porn videos and dreamed of aggressive blonde women with great sexual appetites. They believed porn stars represented the common American woman who was constantly in the state of sexual readiness, and would do exotic things Mexican women would never imagine. That they only needed to find the right way to trigger a gringa's frenzy.

We walked silently. I picked up a seashell and drew a heart in the sand. Susan and Carlos, I wrote. I felt like a caricature of a teenager, like a bikini girl in a Frankie Avalon movie. I didn't care. Carlos drew an arrow through the heart. We walked until a big outcropping of rock stopped us, then we turned back.

Kiss, I wrote in the sand, even though I knew the word in Spanish. *Besar,* Carlos carved with a seashell. He pressed his soft, full lips to mine, sandy fingers at the back of my neck. I tugged his T-shirt out of his pants and urgently ran my hands up his smooth chest. What would he do if I wrestled him to the sand and took his clothes off with my teeth? Would I only prove I was a Vacation Girl, an easy two? Was I not supposed to be, even with my boyfriend? Wasn't four months a long time to go without ever having had sex? I hadn't dated like this since I was a teen. I didn't know the rules.

Love, I wrote, and shivered. Maybe he *did* think of me as a Vacation Girl and love was the furthest thing from his mind. *Amar,* Carlos scratched high up in the packed wet sand, hair fluttering around his cheek. In a flash, I knew that this too-young Mexican boy cared about me a lot, and that I was the one blocking the love. My attitude with guys, since the 1980 incident, had been, you want to love me? You must be stupid.

This felt different though. Maybe I was with Carlos to learn not to deflect men. That was it! I wasn't *supposed* to concentrate on the sex. I was supposed to be learning I could be loved. Maybe I could tell Carlos what I was thinking. But Carlos was looking across the highway to the lit-up motel, where the teachers seemed to be lining up the group out in front.

"We'd better go," he said, holding out his hand. The moment was gone.

There was shuffling and whispers during the night

and a sprawl of girl and boy bodies on the two beds in the morning. Clothed, I was relieved to see. I stepped over empty beer bottles to find my shoes. On the street, the sun warmed the pavement. I found a hotel with fresh flowers in the lobby and sat in the dining room and ordered hot coffee and eggs with frijoles, happy to be free from high school drama. This was the person I was supposed to be—an adult with a newspaper and a meal I could pay for.

Carlos was eating a hot dog from a street cart when I returned, sitting on a low concrete wall that bordered a dried flowerbed. Flashes of my grown-up life zoomed through my head – me doing a standup in front of a camera when I was a news reporter; coffee cups on Jane's kitchen table and smoke curling from the cigarette in her ashtray as we invented dialogue for our screenplay, counting the money in the White Dog Cafe's office at 2 A.M. and placing it carefully in the safe.

My boyfriend held out his hot dog so I could bite it. We crossed the street and sat on the seawall; watching the waves, watching Carlos' classmates throw sand at each other. Areceli, wearing a turquoise bikini, ran squealing, letting Mateo chase her. When he grabbed, she twisted out of the way. Soon, she was absorbed into a circle of girls, unreachable.

"It takes a lot of work, doesn't it?" I mused. Carlos laughed. He'd been watching me watch Araceli.

"Don't they get tired of the games?"

"A few. Why do you think I'm with you?"

Carlos loved the best parts of me. I laughed and jumped off the wall. I began to run down the beach with weightlessness I hadn't felt in years.

HAIRNET

Carlos and Hugo slouched on a green Jardín bench wearing black hairnets, the small knots carefully arranged in the middle of the each forehead. I had almost stepped into the romantic light that lit the Jardín from the Parroquia spires, but stopped short. They looked so comical, I had to hide behind the corn-on-a-stick seller's cart and contemplate a universe in which my boyfriend and his brother looked like Woolworth's grill waitresses. Or gang members. Or convicts.

It was December twenty-third. The duffel bag I'd arrived with was almost packed full, including strings of beaded necklaces from the beach as Christmas presents. The following day, I would drive to San Antonio, Texas with some artist Gussie knew, then fly to Philly.

Earlier, I'd gone to the store for my last bottled Coke. Next to me a guy in baggy shorts lined up a bag of peanuts and two liters of beer on the crowded counter, pulled a roll of US dollars from his pocket and peeled off a ten. He had the kind of haircut the guys in my South Philly neighbor-hood wore, and over his mullet he wore a hair net. Now I got it. The brothers were taking their fashion cues from the guys who'd gone to the States for farm and construction jobs, and roared back into their barrios for Christmas in brand new oversized trucks.

Carlos tugged his hairnet away from his forehead. In Philly, I'd had a thing for motorcycle-jacketed bad boys. I stared from the shadows, trying to see Carlos as a tough guy, but without tattoos and a mean attitude, he only looked like a short order cook.

When I stepped onto the Jardín's paving, Carlos' face lit up.

"Planning on busting out of prison?" I asked as I sat.

"What?" he asked, touching the front knot.

"It's cold," I said, shivering.

"Let's go get warm," Carlos said.

♪♪♪

Just as I was thinking that Christmas break was what I needed to clear my head of a guy who thought the cook-at-the-diner look was happening, Carlos surprised me. He left his hands in his pocket when he kissed me in the doorway the next night, and I turned and put the key in the lock thinking, I'm so *not* going to miss this good-boy-good-girl routine. But when I closed the door behind me, I felt something strange. I turned and stifled a scream. Carlos was in the dark behind me. The velador jumped up from the bench when we walked past.

Inside my apartment, Carlos stood in the middle of the room, shivering in his nubby cotton poncho. When I walked past, he grabbed my hand and pulled me to him with an intensity that made my heart race. Soon we were kissing like Tony and Maria in West Side Story. We fell onto the bed.

I took off my sweater and then, my shirt. Then I started jiggling one leg because all he was doing was looking at me. I ran to the closet and got a sweatshirt and threw it over my head.

"Oye!" Carlos cried from the bed. But he wasn't protesting; he was pointing at something on my chest.

I looked down, tore the sweatshirt off and tossed it away like fish wrapper. Then I went and turned it over so the front of the sweatshirt bearing the words Philadelphia Big Five Hall of Fame and my father's face wouldn't be visible.

"Ooh," I screamed, feigning terror. I launched myself into Carlos' chest. Now that his arms were around my back, he began to fumble with my bra. Inexpertly, was it? Oh, shoot, what if he hadn't done this much before? It made me feel so nervous that I had a realization—I cared. I sucked my breath in. I really cared about this boy who was finally caressing my bare skin.

I turned myself around so I couldn't see my packed bag by the door. Carlos didn't want to see it either. He turned off the table lamp and then lit a candle on the other side, one that only illuminated half the room.

Between heavy curtains, the cold morning sun stretched long ribbons of light into my room. I nestled further into the spoon we made, looking at Carlos' arms wrapped around me, his hand on my hip. I smelled the faint aroma of cologne from his shirt on the floor below. He shifted, pulled me closer, breathed lightly on my shoulder.

While I showered, Carlos warmed tortillas on the gas flame. He split open a black-skinned aguacate and spread its creamy green fruit on the tortillas. We ate them rolled up with cups of instant coffee and milk. At 6:40, he carried my duffel bag outside. He held his hand on my back and I felt like we were the kind of couple who'd already taken several vacations together.

"Pretty soon I'll see how my mother makes me suffer for not coming home."

"You're almost twenty!"

Carlos watched the street for the artist's car.

"You've never spent the night away from home before!"

"She'll have to start getting used to it." If Carlos' hand wasn't on my back, or arm or shoulder, it was on my waist or elbow or hand. He didn't want to let me go. I wasn't sure I was coming back, but he was.

"Have you told your mother about me?" I asked.

"Your name has come up."

"What did you say? Tell me."

Carlos just smiled at me. His mother would hate me. She would smash a Coke bottle against a wall and point it at me if I came to her door. The Parroquia bells chimed 6:45.

"Merry Christmas," I said. To my surprise, my eyes filled with tears. "What are you going to do for Christmas?"

"Nothing."

"Do you give presents?"

Carlos looked at me as if I'd just made a very absurd joke.

"Do you go to church?"

He snorted.

"Um, do you have a tree?" I asked, but I was getting it. Nothing meant they really didn't celebrate. How could I tell him about the mountain of presents, the decorations, the sirloin and cabernet dinner at my parents' house? The mistletoe, the tinsel, the eggnog.

"When you were a kid, did you do anything?"

Carlos looked into the distance. "Once, we got on the bus and went to Queretaro, where my dad was working. We went to one of his friend's houses and there were other kids and two piñatas." He smiled.

"So you had candy from the piñatas? That must have been fun."

"Nuts and oranges. The fun part, though, was all of us being together."

"Right."

We looked at the quiet street.

"You know, that's what it's like for me too. We exchange presents and dress up and go to church but the best part is us being together."

"Go home and tell your mother about me," Carlos said, and then there was a beep, and the Texas artist pulled up in a Mercedes Benz, as if on cue, to remind me of that to which I was supposed to aspire as a good citizen of the United States of America.

///

I drank wine at Christmas dinner in my parents' house and couldn't hold myself back. "He grew up without running water in the house," I whispered to my brothers and sister. "He's never been to a dentist but has perfect teeth!"

"What's going on down there?" my mother asked from behind a pine cone table adornment. We sat twelve at the dining room table set with Mom's good china and Waterford crystal. Bill and Sally's daughter, Chloe squirmed in the high chair we'd used as kids. Paul was down from Boston, where he worked in software. He was considering moving in with his girlfriend. Jen had driven from D.C., where she had a position in renewable energy. She was suffering over a Columbian ex-boyfriend who wouldn't commit, which was usually my position – partnerless at Christmas, and feeling like a freak about it.

"Nothing," I said.

"Sue has a 19-year old boyfriend," my brother Paul supplied.

"Ohhh," my mother groaned.

My father forked up some potatoes and looked at me thoughtfully. My father sold sportswear in Southern Jersey and was home all the time now.

"Is that right, Susan?" asked seventy-one year old Aunt Dorothy.

Six tall tapers burned at each end of the dinner table. My grandfather's brother, Uncle Marty and my Aunt Edna nursed the last of their whiskey Manhattans.

"Rose O'Shea is coming over tomorrow," my mother said brightly. "Kevin asks about you. He's doing quite well selling golf equipment."

"Did you know," Jen asked, "that Mexico is a leading consumer of solar energy panels and equipment?" I looked at her gratefully.

Behind us, the Christmas tree twinkled with white lights and memories. There was the pine cone snowman from my parents' first year of marriage, the angel from the year I was born, a wooden sled I painted when I was eight, a ball that played Silent Night from my Aunt Joan who had died when I was in college. I was surrounded by tradition, in the bosom of my family, where I should feel most at home in the entire world. But I kept thinking of Carlos, who was probably spending Christmas playing basketball. I couldn't explain to anyone how, walking around San Miguel with Carlos next to me, I didn't feel like a nervous wreck of a person any more. Susan and Kevin O'Shea the golf pro. That's what they wanted. Kevin O'Shea and his pals and their wives in their pearl necklaces. I longed to feel the sun on my face.

"That's what I call a good meal," Uncle Marty said, sitting back.

I jumped up to clear plates. In the kitchen Jen and Paul arranged the Christmas cookies on a plate, and I made coffee.

"When he was twelve, Carlos had a job walking a drunken neighbor home from a cantina every night," I said. I couldn't help bringing him up.

Jen's mouth dropped open.

"Just your style, someone comfortable in bars," Paul smirked.

I probably should have kept quiet, but the idea that I was *supposed* to made me mad. I had one big secret—the Player and the Agent—I'd never told the family. That was difficult enough. Now I wasn't supposed to talk about a kind boy who cared about me? I was getting grumpy. Then I remembered I had a kind and decent boy who cared about me.

"Susan," my father said, back at the table, pushing aside his dessert plate, "going out with a student is not, em...professional."

"Nothing about that school is professional," I laughed.

"Then why are you going back there?"

I had announced that I would, that I had to finish teaching. I let them think I had a contract. But the answer was clear, and worrisome, to everybody. I was going back for Carlos.

///

On December 31st, I went to the White Dog Cafe's New Year's Eve party in Philadelphia.

"Do you do the Cucaracha down there?" asked Gary, my former bar manager.

New Year's Eve the year before, the waitresses, including me, had danced on the bar, late, while the cooks sat on bar chairs below looking up our dresses. John, a St. Joseph's University student who worked as a busboy, had brought his roommate.

"Those women have beards under their arms," the

roommate squawked. "Let's get out of here!" But when two waitresses started dancing and grinding with each other, they had remained at a bar table watching, mouth open, and clutching their tap beers until the foamy heads disappeared.

After that, I ran out onto snow-covered sidewalk to get some dance tapes from my car. St. Joe's John tapped on the passenger side window and jumped in when I pulled the lock. I knew John's type. I had the perverted impulse to push John out of his Irish Catholic box where he went to Mass, spoke nicely to his mother, thumbed dirty magazines in his bedroom, drank Rolling Rock beer, and dated girls who wore gold crosses on chains.

He couldn't get a handle on me—I could see it. My dad was a legend at his school, and here I was, a former Catholic school good girl who lived in a black and Korean neighborhood and who bought cute underwear at a discount shop and then displayed it to the wait staff while it was on me. I let John untuck his shirt and show me his Christmas tree boxer shorts because he was not only uptight but cute. We steamed the windows for a couple of minutes before we patted our hair into place and returned to the party.

John didn't work at the White Dog any more, and I didn't ask about him.

A year ago, I had been dancing and grinding on the bar in a tiny black velvet cocktail dress. The waitresses were up there now. Jessica was taking off her dress, like she did when she got drunk. Tim, an art student who looked like a frat boy, had Melanie pressed up against the grill.

"Don't you want to be my white Christmas, Susan?" asked black Freddie in a Santa hat.

I only wanted to be with Carlos. The bus boys didn't look half as cute any more. I didn't want to kiss anyone at midnight, and I didn't.

///

"Susan, you could get a graduate degree from Temple," my mother said. She wiped down her kitchen counter for the second time with 409.

My former bar manager had said he couldn't promise Saturdays, but could give me some hours. I sipped coffee, pretending to read the paper. My bed was still at Joy's house. She'd been using my car for six months. I *could* easily slip back into my life.

When I realized my plane ticket was lost, and with it, the guarantee I would see Carlos in four days, I stopped thinking about my furniture, my job, my car. I stopped eating. I took a bus to Jane's house in South Philly because American Airlines said I had to go into its Market Street office to get a new ticket. My car wore a film of old snow and street salt. I urged it through the streets, parked it on Walnut and rushed inside with Christmas money from Uncle Marty and Aunt Edna.

I would have a new ticket in three days. I went back to Jane's house in South Philly – the closest place I knew to the airport. Christmas trees draped in sad tinsel listed on curbs. Inside, I switched channels, washed and folded laundry.

"We're having Mary Frances's birthday party here on Saturday. Stay!" Jane said. Last year's party had started late in the afternoon and by midnight included Mr. Love from across the street who wanted to dance with the white girls, and a few Mummers who looked like they'd been drunk since the New Year's Day parade.

I called Gussie in San Miguel.

"Can you find Carlos and tell him I'll be three days late?" I pleaded.

"Sure. Where does he live?"

I'd known Carlos for four months. "I don't know," I said.

///

In San Miguel, I threw my bags inside the apartment and race-walked to the Jardín. It was almost eight by the Parroquia clock. Carlos was sitting alone on a bench facing the portales where my mother and I had clapped along with the mariachis two months earlier. He was hunched into his heavy cotton poncho, hands in the front pockets.

Carlos' posture straightened when he saw me. He jerked his head to the right and began to walk. I followed him across the Jardín and down Calle Hidalgo until he stepped into the deep alcove of a darkened doorway. There in the dark he pulled me to him, cheek pressed hard against the top of my head. Pedestrians with scarves wrapped around their necks hurried by in the chilly night.

In San Miguel, Carlos had endured a rough ten days. In front of his sister's house, he kicked gravel with his toe. "Moping over your gringa?" his sister smirked.

"Where did your gringa go?" his father asked him. Carlos' mother shook her head at him.

"Get used to it. She's not coming back," Hugo had laughed.

In the doorway, Carlos took in big deep breaths then released them against my hair. I remained crushed into his body, my face against the knobby cotton. He smelled of soap and the cold. Finally he pulled back and pushed his hair away from his face with his wrist, or, in the dark I could not tell, was he wiping away a tear?

BAD NEIGHBORHOOD

"I see things," Carlos said a few nights later. We were walking in Guadiana, past the park. "I see us on a street in San Miguel with a child."

"What do you mean you see things?"

"You know."

"No, I have no idea."

"I get vibes about things that are going to happen."

"You mean like Tales from the Dark Side or something?" I imagined Christopher, the guy my sister was dating, sitting over his financial charts. He'd be wearing his you're-shitting-me look by now.

"Boy or girl? What else? Am I going to stay here?"

"You really want to know?"

"Yes! Would you consult your internal crystal ball or something?"

Carlos laughed.

I see us with a child. What kind of guy said stuff

like that? Funny thing was, it didn't seem like a party trick coming from Carlos. It was like he really believed what he was saying.

///

The bartender held his hands together over his head and moved his hips in a circle.

"He used to be an exotic dancer in Arizona," Amber sighed, leaning on her elbow. Amber told me Nancy had forgiven the loutish teenagers for Thanksgiving. That was to convince me to go to Mama Mia's for drinks.

"I ended up in his apartment one night," Amber said when the bartender turned to mix margaritas. I had just moved in with her. The ceramics teacher had returned to claim the apartment I'd been occupying. I would stay with Amber next door for two weeks, then, move up to the far side of town with Gussie.

"First just a backrub, he didn't want to do anything, but then, you know, with the Gypsy Kings playing, he couldn't resist." She sighed and switched elbows.

"What about your boyfriend in Baltimore?" I asked, sipping a Corona.

"Did I tell you he's Iranian?"

"A dozen times."

"He's still there, managing the pizza place. He's so far away." Amber held her third shot of tequila between two fingers. Her eyelids drooped as she stared at the bartender, who unloaded a bucket of cubes into the ice bin.

A dark, chiseled-cheeked man leaned against the back wall, smoking cigarettes. "That's Eric," Amber said. "He's here with pot for the band." Eric's bored stance shifted every time a gringa walked in. Next thing we knew, he was standing behind us, draping an arm around Amber and whispering into her ear.

"Yeah, a small bag," Amber replied. "Maybe a little extra for a little extra."

"I've got to do some business first," Eric said and disappeared.

"God, could be trouble if Saturnino shows up tonight," she muttered.

"Who's Saturnino?"

"A ranchero. He comes in his truck and brings me pot. Sweet guy. Big shoulders."

Eric walked us home, squeezing Amber by the shoulder on one side, grabbing at my waist on the other while I twisted away from him in a crazy dance down Calle Jesús.

In the house, Amber and Eric built a small pyramid of pot at the tiled kitchen counter and busied themselves with rolling papers. I went up to my room, separated from Amber's room by only a curtain. Soon footsteps stumbled up the stairs, then Amber shrieked and her bed creaked loudly. I put a pillow over my head but it didn't shut out the giggles.

Fifteen minutes later, the screen door downstairs whined and banged shut. Half an hour later, it opened again. Heavy steps on the staircase, a deep voice speaking Spanish, and the air thickening again with the odor of dope. I opened my window to the cold night air, strained for the sound of church bells. My breath made little clouds over the blankets.

Tap, tap, tap. Pebbles on my window. Carlos stood below, his bright white jeans luminous in the moonlight.

"You made friends with the *pistolero*?" I asked, then pulled my head in and closed the window.

Carlos' friends were still warning him about me—American women used drugs at parties and were easy to take home.

Downstairs, I held the screen door so it wouldn't creak, and pulled my sweatshirt hood up. I crossed the courtyard to the fountain and sat on its cold concrete edge. Carlos stood before me, bouncing from foot to foot.

"The velador says men have been coming in and out all night." A worried crease puckered the skin between Carlos's eyes.

"Amber."

"Not you, right?"

"No," I said in an of-course-not voice. "The guys bring her pot."

Carlos looked around.

"Do you? You know, like pot?"

"I don't like pot and I don't like having more than one boyfriend."

Carlos' forehead uncreased. "But you've tried it." He frowned again.

"Carlos, trying marijuana was part of going to college." I thought of Kevin O'Shea, the golf equipment salesman. Would I fit better into a life with someone like him? I searched my brain for common ground with Carlos.

"It's cold. Don't you want to go in?" Carlos asked.

"She's got some ranchero in there."

"We'll be quiet."

I shrugged and walked to the door, forgetting to make it not creak. Upstairs, we got into bed with our clothes on. I faced Carlos, snuggled my head into his shoulder. He put my hands into his front pocket, and wrapped an arm around me, pulling me close. From Amber's room came light snoring.

Just before I slept, it occurred to me I felt safe. I didn't have to trade anything back to be with Carlos. Did he feel safe too? Maybe that was all we had in common. Maybe it was enough.

My new house atop Calle Independencia was on the north edge of town, up a hill, with a view. Gussie had found the house. It had one empty upstairs room to house her canvases for painting, and another for the Mexican-themed magnets and frames she was making and exporting. The brick homes lining the street had small windows and metal and curtain doors. Tin *chile en vinagre* cans bursting with geraniums were nailed to the outside walls. Neighbors sat on brick piles or lounged in doorways, watching Gussie and me move in my word processor, her paints.

Carlos and Hugo came over the rise as we struggled with a large plant in a big clay pot, carrying a table on their heads, kicking a soccer ball back to a young boy on the street.

Gussie and I led the boys to the kitchen, and they put the table next to a wall sponge-painted sunset pink. Gussie turned over two orange crates for seats and stuck a spray of wildflowers in a Coke bottle.

"This is a bad neighborhood," Carlos said, looking out the second-story window. "And look, this is the only house with a second floor. You know what that means."

"That we have to climb stairs?"

"You're the house everyone wants to rob. Plus, didn't you see that band of marijuanos on the corner?" Outside Jane's house in South Philly, the sidewalk was sometimes littered with crack vials. A man had been shot to death across the street a few weeks before I left for Mexico. Drug deal gone bad, the neighbors said. I'd laid in bed reading and heard the muffled pop-pop, like the report from a clogged tailpipe. Carlos thought I shouldn't be living among robbers and potheads. But the house was large and quiet.

"The rent is cheap. Where do you want me to live?" I asked, slightly annoyed.

///

In the yard, half a dozen fruit trees stretched their fuzzy green limbs in the sun. Gussie was convinced that the only thing our palace lacked was animals.

"Gussie wants a chicken," I told Carlos.

Two days later, a short handsome, familiar-looking woman knocked on our door. She had a baby suspended at her breast in an intricately wrapped rebozo and two small children by the hand.

"Hola," I said. A pretty girl about six years old peeked from behind her skirt, then looked at the floor when I smiled at her.

"*No esta Carlos?*" the mother asked.

"No, Carlos isn't here." Suddenly I recognized my boyfriend in her face.

"It's Carlos' sister!" I whispered to Gussie. "What do I do with her?" I smiled at the younger child, who buried her face in her mother's skirt.

"*Quieres ver la casa?*" I offered. Do you want to see the house?

"Uh-oh," I said to Gussie, "I addressed her in the familiar. Should I have used *Usted?*"

"She looks younger than us. I think you did all right."

I gave them a tour of empty rooms, following the aquamarine and white floor tiles upstairs and down again, ending in the kitchen. I searched for a conversation-starter. "*Gussie quiere animales.*"

"Yeah, I want a chicken," Gussie admitted. Mariana looked around at the frying pan, a bag of Bimbo bread, a returnable Coke bottle. Then she picked up a broom and with children still attached to her body, began to sweep the floor.

I looked at Gussie, startled.

"Mariana, no."

"Hey, come on, we'll clean up later," Gussie supplied while I tried to figure out why Carlos' sister would knock on my door and sweep my kitchen. Did Mariana think our house was dirty? Did she work as a maid and couldn't help picking up a broom? Did she want a job? Was she nervously covering an awkward pause in a conversation that couldn't go much further because our Spanish was limited?

Soon, she propped the broom in the corner and, children still clinging to her like a fairy tale mother, she left.

The following day, the doorbell sounded. This time Mariana stood alone, a burlap frijol bag in her hand. The bag suddenly leapt away from her body.

"*Tu pollo*," she said.

She held the bag open and I looked inside. A small white chicken stared back, opening its beak. "Gussie!" I called into the house.

"*Pásale*," I said. No, Mariana said, she didn't want to come in. But she remained in the doorway.

"Maybe we're supposed to pay her," said Gussie, at my side.

"*Cuanto?*" I asked.

"*Veinte-cinco pesos.*"

"I'll pay," said Gussie.

"Well, I don't want the damn thing."

When Gussie gave her 25 pesos, Mariana slipped her hand under her T-shirt and pushed around under her bra. Her hand came back out empty. Her smile was like Carlos', a sudden sunburst lighting up her solemn face.

"*Ya me voy,*" she said. I watched her back as she walked up the cobblestone street, childless arms swinging.

"Look, it's so cute," Gussie cooed, peering into the bag.

"What does it eat?" I asked.

"You got me."

The chicken wandered around the yard, bobbing its head at the lime trees, the insects in the grass, our hot water heater that never kept its flame since we were at the top of a windy hill. It hopped onto a stack of soda bottle crates that came with the house. Gussie followed it rapturously.

Gussie brought home a street dog. She brought home a Frenchman who spoke Spanish with a strange hiss on his s's. The Frenchman was a young architect, touring Mexico before he returned to work in France–which I didn't believe when he moved in because he didn't have a place to stay. And ate our food. And asked for money because he had run out.

///

"Where are the eggs?" Gussie cried a few days later. The chicken roosted among the soda bottles at night and Gussie checked every morning for eggs. I wrinkled my nose and stepped around one of the dozen slippery piles of *mierda* the chicken left on the back patio.

"Where are the eggs?" Gussie asked Carlos, when he came over after working in his brother-in-law's tin shop.

"This chicken is a baby. It won't have eggs for a few more months."

"Oh," said Gussie sadly. Then she brightened. "A baby!" She ran clucking after the chicken, determined to coax affection from it. The chicken careened around the yard on spindly legs.

"Don't have many chickens where she's from?" Carlos asked, shaking his head.

"Chicago? Not that don't come wrapped in cellophane."

"We've always had chickens," he said.

Another clue. He had a fierce mother and chickens and a pretty sister with kids.

At dusk, we sat on the windy roof of the house, crosslegged on cement that warmed our legs, releasing the day's heat as it cooled. Lights blinked on up and down the hill and dotted the tops of steeples as night cloaked the city. Gussie and the Frenchman were out to dinner. Supposedly he was treating.

"I don't want to go home," Carlos said, flinging pebbles over the roof ledge. "My mother and sister are fighting."

"Which sister?"

"Dulce."

"How old's Dulce?"

"Twenty-five."

"What are they fighting about?"

"They just always fight. They yell a lot."

"Well, what does Dulce do?"

"What do you mean, do?"

"You know, work?"

"Nothing. She stays in the house."

"All day?"

"She goes out to get tortillas."

"But what does she *do?*" I had been a television news reporter at age twenty-five. I jogged and cross-country skied, planned dinners with friends, rented movies, got my hair cut and colored, drank local beer.

"She cleans the floors. Sometimes makes the meals. My mother leaves her money to buy food, and then tells her she buys the wrong things. She and Dulce scream at each other. Then my brother, Gerónimo, gets mad and leaves. Stays out all night. That makes my mother mad too."

"How old is Gerónimo?"

Carlos thought. "Twenty three?"

"And what does he do?"

"He sleeps."

"Come on."

"He sleeps all day. That's what he does. He gets up in the afternoon, eats, gets mad if there's no meal made, showers and goes out at night."

"He doesn't work?"

"No."

"He doesn't go to school?"

Carlos shook his head and studied a scar on his arm.

"I'd make your brother and sister go out and get a job."

"Ha! Just try."

Maybe they all just needed some Dear Abby advice. "Can't your mother get tough and say, 'No freeloading around here?'" Couldn't she back herself up with a weapon, I thought but didn't say.

Carlos laughed. There was probably something I wasn't getting culturally here. But, *chispas*, we were all human beings, weren't we? How much different could our families really be?

THE LAMINA-ROOFED HOUSE

Sunday mornings, teenagers in knock-off Nikes played basketball on the Benito Juarez Park courts. Pre-teens circled on bicycles. Agua vendors set up pot-bellied glass barrels of watermelon, lime and tamarind water. Carlos and I sat on a low wall. I swung my legs.

"What?" I said. Carlos was sneaking glances my way without turning his head.

"*Nada*," he said. A women's game began on court one. Carlos put his hand on my knee and squeezed until my kneecap twitched. He watched an outside shot that went *swish*. He looked at me, studying my face.

"*What?*"

We watched the basketball game some more. It was March. The day was heating up early. Jacaranda trees were in the first of their bloom, fragrant purple clouds waving behind brick walls. I'd been in San Miguel ten months.

"Do you want to go to my house?" Carlos asked with the suddenness of a quickened heartbeat.

"Sí," I answered, jumping from the wall, my sandals sending up puffs of park dust as I landed. Yes.

From the park, we walked to the outdoor market at the San Antonio church. The rich golden odor of pork filled the air. *Carnitas*-sellers poured pig fat into emptied chili cans that the buyers brought from their homes, and weighed it for sale. At a huge rectangular table heaving under mountains of fruit, I stopped to examine sunset-colored mangos. A short woman in a Get Wired T-shirt was reaching for a cantaloupe, pressing its ends with her thumb, lifting it to her face to judge the aroma. She turned to hand the melon to the vendor to weigh, and saw us.

"Ma," Carlos said.

Her face was plump and pretty, and her smile, radiant in a way I had never imagined. She was young. I'd imagined an old crone in a rebozo and house apron tied behind her back with a no-nonsense yank, thick legs set apart while she stared me down. Instead, she wore polka-dotted cotton pants. Her dark girlish hair was held behind her ears with bobby pins. She smoothed loose strands away from her face.

"*Ella es Susana*," Carlos said. He held my hand tightly. Levi's, a yellow scallop-necked cotton T-shirt, Italian leather sandals I'd found at the Tuesday Market, blondish hair growing out. My aggressive downtown look was gone. Still, I didn't look like other girls at this outdoor market, with their baskets of homemade tortillas and black hair waterfalling down their backs.

"I'm Juana," Carlos' mother said. "Look," she said, as if I were a neighbor. "The melons are good and juicy today." All the nights her son spent in my house instead of hers—she could hate me. But Juana was smiling at me. I smiled back.

"We're going to the house, Ma," Carlos informed.

"*Andale*. I'm going to make mole." She piled black-red

chiles on the scale, then slipped her hand under her T-shirt, withdrew money and handed it to the same fruit vendor I used to buy from when I was teaching at the Prepa. His hair was uncombed but the shirt he usually wore inside-out was on right. Juana held her mesh bag open by the handles, and he loaded in fruit, tomatoes and chiles, and then threw in a bunch of cilantro.

"*Un pilón*," he said, scratching his head. A little bonus. He used to give me an apple.

"Take these," she said. From her plastic mesh bag she withdrew a bag of strawberries. I accepted the plump fruit, and Carlos took his mother's heavy shopping bag.

"I'm going to buy chicken. See you at home," Juana said. She waved at us, and smiled again. She hadn't seemed surprised to meet me.

We continued through the market, past cheap plastic toys hanging from poles, beans and rice in pyramids on tarps on the ground, an old man on a three-legged stool selling ceramic cups and bowls.

Yellow sunlight heated the stones under our feet. We walked down streets I'd never seen before, even in running. The strawberries began to bleed in the bag. My hands and head were sweating, but I felt light, like I had reached a watershed, passed a test.

At the end of a street called *Jesus, Maria y José*, a large drainpipe ran under the road. The mouth of the drainpipe was clogged with rotting wood and crumpled Sabritas bags. There, we turned left and descended a rocky hill. Carlos pointed to the middle of the hill. A brick exterior, a corrugated plastic roof. Lamina. What people who couldn't afford cement used. His house.

Although I kept my head straight, my eyes darted left and right as our feet carefully stepped over rocks and gullies left by rain. Neighbors appeared in doorways and windows, watching our descent. A girl about Carlos' age stood holding a broom handle on a cement stoop. Her poly-blend sweatpants shone in the sun and her T-shirt was big enough to fit my father. Aside from my fair skin and hair, blue eyes and halting Spanish, my clothes alone set me apart from the people on the hill. At the outdoor markets, I spotted the good cotton, the reinforced seam, the quality shoe-leather like my mother taught me.

One lady, staring from a doorway, wore rubber shoes with little raised rubber stitches around the edges that cost three dollars in the stores on Calle Insurgentes, a step up from the pink plastic slip-ons that cost a dollar fifty. Her T-shirt read, I Did It My Way. When I told my students to work on their own, they looked at me blankly, and then continued calling answers to one another. Sometimes I thought they understood teamwork better than me, the coach's daughter.

Sticker bushes thrust long spiky branches into the path, catching my pant legs. I held my boyfriend's hand so I wouldn't stumble.

In the middle of the hill, I spotted a half dozen corn stalks and a jumble of flowering plants growing under a window that had Kellogg's Corn Flakes boxes in the panes instead of glass. We stepped under a small brick arch over which perched a concrete eagle with blue marbles for eyes. Following a narrow passage lined with round hand-formed windows, I glimpsed a bed in a dark room.

Two chickens scurried past us and out the front door. I stepped over a pile of chicken mierda, and thought of how one of my mother's most trying chores had always been keeping our house germ-free. When I thought of my mother, disinfectant sprays, sparkling counters and spotless floors came to mind. At the end of the passage was a wild tumble of plants in large chile en vinagre cans. I followed Carlos as he stepped onto the small patio.

Stairs led from a tiny cement patio, two sets going up

and one going down. Poinsettias grew in a concrete planter that edged the down stairs. The planter also served as a waste receptacle. I tried not to stare at the sucked mango stone, the gum wrapper, a pink hairbrush with squashed-down bristles and pieces of wire in the dirt under a large red bloom. A drain defined the middle of the tiny patio floor. Next to it, where someone had aimed and missed, was a gob of spit. I recoiled, feeling like I was in my mother's body. Walking through this house so far was like stepping in a minefield. Carlos didn't seem to notice the trash or body fluids.

Birdcages lined the brick patio walls. Under the cages on the left wall stood a round concrete sink, the spigot of which was the penis of a small concrete boy who reclined against the brick, pissing. It was an accomplished sculpture, reminding me of cherubs in Italian fountains except for the flat Aztec cheeks and indigenous nose.

"Carlos," I whispered. We stood in the middle of the patio. "Where did that sink come from?"

"My father made it. He made the eagle over the front door too."

Next to the boy-peeing sink was the doorless entrance to a sinkless kitchen. Flies buzzed in a clump at the doorway. The lingering aroma of mashed frijoles and heated tortillas drifted from the kitchen. By the stove, a solidly round girl in a skirt, T-shirt and rubber sandals was sweeping a pile of orange rinds onto the edge of a torn milk carton. She was darker than Carlos. Her unsmiling eyes were black and almost perfectly almond-shaped like his. Her T-shirt had red stains and a large rip under the right breast. The broom stopped its scritch, scritch, and the girl watched me. I smiled. "Hola," I said. The girl flicked her ponytail over her shoulder and lowered her head to her sweeping. A chill crept up my neck.

A powerfully built man pushed aside a blanket that

covered the doorway to the upper room. He was larger than Carlos and wore sweatpants and a T-shirt with the collar ripped away. Large, cracked hands lifted a mesh baseball cap and pushed unruly black hair under it. His fingers were so thick I wondered if his wife had to cut his food for him. Carlos' father, the great concrete artist. He stepped back and let the blanket fall when he saw me.

My father would have stridden across a room, hand out, if a newcomer stepped into our home. A man would get a slap on the back; a woman would be shown to a chair. My father had worked in the glare of arena spotlights and television cameras, argued with referees, made himself indifferent to the roar of cheering and booing fans.

"Why won't anyone speak to me?" I whispered to Carlos.

"Eh, that's how they are," Carlos replied, squeezing my shoulder. "My father doesn't talk to anyone until he knows them really well."

I felt my sunburned skin, my beauty shop haircut. I felt the hundred-peso bill in my pocket. I stood, a weak smile on my face.

When we'd gone to Laberintos, Carlos had paid. He wore a leather-trimmed jacket. I never imagined he lived in a house with unfinished brick walls and doorways with no doors. A large refrigerator took up one side of the kitchen and I thought it must speak of some level of income, but just then the sister in the ponytail opened one of its double doors and I saw it was filled with tin dishes and plastic bags.

"*Tu mamá?*" the father asked from the shadows.

"My mother is buying fruit in the *plazita*. She's going to the *pollería*," Carlos answered. I remembered the mother and my shoulders relaxed. She had turned her smile on me like a beam of light. In a curled fist with fingernails digging into my palm, I held the plastic bag she had given me, filled with strawberries—red, juicy and dripping sweetly onto my shoe.

I followed Carlos as he descended the down staircase. He opened the door to a dark room. A blanket tacked to the ground level window blocked the daylight. There was nobody in the room, but the television was on, its blue glow, the room's only light. Three beds lined the exposed brick walls. A polyester spread adorned with ladies with pink parasols covered the corner bed. Carlos smoothed the bedspread on the bed opposite the television and plumped up a paisley pillow. I leaned back. Into lumps.

"What's in here?"

"Old clothes," Carlos replied.

"Someone tied them into knots before stuffing them inside?"

It was cool in the room, cave-like and cozy. The day's heat remained outside the covered window; an old Mexican movie played on the television. A *charro*, a fancy cowboy, rode across an expansive property to declare himself to the hacienda owner's daughter, a black haired beauty in the kind of gathered, low cut blouse worn by Chi Chi's Mexican restaurant hostesses. I tried to follow the dialogue but already didn't like the woman's supplicating hands. Carlos climbed onto the bed, stuck another lumpy pillow behind his back and put one arm behind his head. He had probably watched TV on this bed in that position for years.

"Who sleeps here?" I asked.

"Hugo, me and Dulce."

In the dark, he could not see my eyebrows shooting up in surprise.

"How do you all, you know, change your clothes?"

"When you shower."

Slow footsteps came down the steps and Carlos' mother, Juana entered the room. Earth-brown skin, a few gray hairs. There were probably fewer years between me and her than between me and her son. She carried two ceramic bowls with spoons.

We took the bowls and spooned up fresh mango and yogurt. The bed springs creaked when Juana sat on the bed across from us.

"It's very good," I said.

"*Se hace el yogurt con bulguras.*"

I smiled. "What?" I whispered to Carlos.

"She makes the yogurt herself," he told me in Spanish, which I understood.

"*Ya me voy.*" Juana walked like my Uncle Crash, who'd suffered a knee injury playing football fifty years ago and still moved by swinging his left leg out to the side.

"What's wrong with her legs?"

"Arthritis or something. She's gone to every *curandera* in the barrio. They've tried herbs, candles, bee stings, rubbing garlic on her knees. Sometimes the cures work for a little while, but the pain always comes back."

A boy of about four came into the room and sat on the bed across from us, staring as we ate. I elbowed Carlos.

"That boy is Miguel, my brother, Gerónimo's son. He and his little brother and their mother live here."

Three more people in this house? I hadn't seen more bedrooms.

"Your brother is married?"

"No."

"But he has a whole family living in this house."

"Sí."

"Who was that in the kitchen?"

"Dulce."

I sank back into the lumpy pillow. The cowboy on TV was having a gun battle with a mustachioed guy in a big hat.

"How…?"

"Gerónimo is not a very attentive father and Lupe

sleeps a lot so my mother likes to watch over the boys," Carlos said as the cowboy swaggered across the screen with exaggerated machismo. "They don't always eat when they're in Lupe's house."

"Does Lupe work?"

"No."

"Gerónimo and Lupe don't work?" Carlos concentrated on the death of the bad guy on the screen. My head began to hurt. Just as my eyes closed I smelled food. Juana shuffled into the room with two plastic plates of chicken and rice covered with a thick brown sauce and topped with raw onion rings.

"It smells heavenly!" I said as I accepted the plate. There was no fork. I copied Carlos, tearing off a chunk of chicken with tortilla, dipping the wrapped chicken in mole and popping the whole piece in my mouth.

"My mother has worked as a cook in a couple of gringo houses," Carlos said.

"Lucky them," I said. "What's in the sauce?" I asked Juana while she sat there watching us.

"Chocolate, chile, banana and nuts among other ingredients," Juana replied.

"Where's the hairbrush, '*mano*?" Dulce asked, entering and sneaking glances at me as she searched a stack of shelves made of scrap wood.

"*Quien sabe*," Carlos replied. Who knows?

An overweight young woman dressed in thin striped cotton pants with a hole in the knee and battered yellow high-heeled shoes entered next. Her short hair was permed to the texture of a scrubbing pad and her brown cheeks savagely rouged. She placed two green glass bottles of Coke next to the bed.

"Ha, ha. Lupe put on makeup because you're here," Carlos said when she'd gone. He rummaged in the alcove behind the bed, pulled out a belt and popped the caps off with the buckle. The Coke was cold and sweet. The sun's gold deepened at the edge of the window. Carlos put his arm around my waist when everybody left and pulled me close. I spooned into him. The television droned.

The sun was gone when I awoke, the blanket in the window edged in a dusky blue light. Someone had covered me with mosquito netting. I sat on the bed looking at a concrete cross, built in relief in the wall over Dulce's bed. It was about three feet high and two feet across—a simple cross but for the oversized hands protruding from the ends—the thick-fingered hands of the concrete artist who made it. The crosses of my youth—over the altar in St. Dorothy's church, above the blackboard of every class I attended for ten years, on the rosaries clicking softly at the nuns' sides—all came with a suffering Jesus on them. This figureless cross with its joyous open hands seemed to come from some happy form of Catholicism I didn't know.

"I'm so embarrassed," I said when Carlos flicked on the overhead light bulb. "I slept for hours."

"I think you're sick. You need to stay here and get well." He pushed the hair back from my face.

Ooh, I wanted to be sick. I wanted his cool hand on my forehead all day long. Maybe I *was* sick. I sat up. I had classes to give, obligations.

"I have to go home." Why did I have to be so American?

We walked down Calle Orizaba holding hands. "So, was it terrible having me in your house?" Older couples were out on front steps in the warm evening. Little girls in flouncy princess dresses slurped popsicles. They stared as we passed and made me remember what we looked like— my pale hand in Carlos' brown one.

"No." Carlos smiled. "Now I want you to come and spend the night."

"No way. I'll end up like Lupe. She came to stay one

night and now she's fat and jobless."

"I want you with me."

"I can't spend the night. Then I won't be able to leave and go back to my life," I said, making a joke out of what I felt. But I knew I would go back to the house and sleep on an old-clothes pillow. I would tell myself it was about seeing how the strange family who all slept together lived. A social experiment. But the truth was I was riding on a whooshing love train and it was picking up speed. Going to sleep and waking again with my entire body pressed up next to Carlos' was a narcotic. If Carlos had said, let's sleep at the top of the Parroquia, I would have said, bring me a blanket. Weren't the outstretched arms and open hands of the cross on the downstairs wall waiting to welcome me again?

LA CHIONA

"There's like a million people in the house, and there are only two rooms besides the kitchen!" I said. Gussie sat on an orange crate in the kitchen, sipping a XX lager. The Frenchman snored in her bedroom above.

"I keep waiting for this to wear off, but you're serious about this guy, aren't you?"

I sighed, looked at her, my hands full of dish soap. "It's just so simple with him. He likes me, and he lets me know it every day. No games."

"Two rooms and no games. I hope you know what you're in for."

Two nights later, Carlos held my hand as we descended the rocky path toward a single light that burned in the card-boarded kitchen window of the tiny lamina-roofed house.

Downstairs, we watched *Dos Mujeres, Un Camino*—Two Women, One Road—the nighttime soap, *la telenovela,* that played on all the TVs in all the one-room stores in the neighborhood. Former CHiPS actor Eric Estrada had

had to learn Spanish for his role as Johnny, a nice-guy truck driver in love with his wife and a curvy teenaged nymph at the same time.

I sat cross-legged in overalls, grading papers. We leaned against the lumpy pillows on Carlos' single bed, alone in the downstairs room. The family was watching *Dos Mujeres* on the upstairs TV. Carlos' thumb went da-dum, da-dum on my leg. Johnny was having a clandestine meeting with his teenage girlfriend, who gazed at him with sad, soulful eyes.

Just as Johnny was explaining how he couldn't leave his wife, over swooning background music, the bed began to shake. "Yo, quit jiggling. I can't write," I said, but Carlos wasn't moving. He was still and alert, as if listening for deer in the woods. Then the floor rumbled, the stereo began to tremble and one by one two small porcelain vases—favors from two *quinceaños* parties Dulce had attended—crashed to the floor.

"Earthquake!" I said.

"We're safe down here." The walls and the ceiling of the lower room were made of poured concrete. Carlos ran to the door. "*Venganse!*" But before anybody could answer, the earth's movement stopped.

Upstairs, minutes later, the parakeets were silent under the laundry that topped their cages. Carlos picked up a crumpled tube of toothpaste and shook it free of bird food. The night-blooming jasmine spilling from a large boot glue can smelled like honey. Stars twinkled over my head and it was hard to tell the earth had just grumbled.

Light suddenly flooded the patio. In the kitchen, Carlos' father, Maximo, finished screwing a light bulb into a cord hanging from the ceiling. Ceramic dishware lay shattered on the floor.

"La Chiona is really angry tonight. I'm not going to get any sleep," Maximo mumbled, retrieving pieces of a soup bowl from the tiled sink.

Maximo *did* speak.

I knew the legend of La Llorona, the Mexican woman who had drowned her own children and was doomed to wander through eternity, crying for them.

"We call the Wailing Woman in our house La Chiona," Carlos explained, as I brushed bird food off the sink ledge.

"She's been in this house ever since I built it," Maximo said. "This land must have been haunted since your grandfather donated it to your mother. No wonder he gave it away."

I covered my mouth. Carlos saw my raised eyebrows. "She makes noise," Carlos explained. "She bangs pans and scrapes spoons on bowls in the kitchen. Moves around in the bedrooms too, kicks shoes, bumps into the beds."

"All the time?" I sputtered.

"Every couple of weeks," Maximo said, picking up pieces of shattered ceramic.

"She bothers my father more than anyone."

"Never had a good man in her life. That's what she's crying about," Maximo said.

"Once, when I was about ten, my friend Leslie Schellhouse was spending the night. We heard an eerie wailing. It turned out to be a cat," I said weakly.

"This one doesn't let me sleep, but she's not as bad as the witches," Maximo said.

"Witches. Heh-heh," I laughed. Maximo did not smile.

"I was always afraid for you kids when the witches were around," Juana said from the upstairs doorway. It came out muffled; she was pulling a poncho over her head. On her feet were a Hello Kitty sock and a man's brown sock, creased where her toes had slid into rubber flip flops.

"They left me at the top of a tree when I was two,"

Maximo said. He took a carton of milk from the refrigerator door. My head swiveled back and forth.

"Over in the hills, where Malanquin is now, before there were any houses, is where the witches used to gather," Juana said, taking a broom from the corner. "We lived on Canal. I would see them with their lanterns at night from my window. Most of them were the ones that turn into balls of fire. They fly, you know. They sell themselves to the devil for wings."

"Witches in San Miguel? How can you tell who they are?" I gasped.

"In the day time, they just look like señoras." Juana swept the pieces of a mayonnaise jar that had held salt into a pile. "But at night they sprout their wings, get wild eyes and fly around doing no good at all. Sometimes I saw balls of fire shooting up over the hills."

Taking a paper bag of pan de *azucar* from the top of the refrigerator, she handed Maximo a sugary croissant. Bags of sugar, rice, lentils, and frijoles had been jolted from where they'd been piled on the refrigerator. They crashed onto the table where crusty *bolillo*, garlic bulbs, a bag of salt, red and green tomatoes, guayabas, and a bottle of San Luis salsa already made their home. "Ay, Viejo, when are you going to build me a counter?" Juana sighed, filling a pot with water from the pissing boy sink.

"How did you get left in a tree?" I asked Máximo.

"I was two years old," he said, wiping crumbs from his chin. One night around three A.M. my mother found me sitting way up at the top of the tree in our yard."

"How did you get up there?" I asked.

Isn't it obvious, his look said.

"Witches left you up there?" I asked.

Maximo shrugged.

I turned to Juana, who was splitting open half a dozen yellow guayabas and putting them in the water. "So, what happened to the ball-of-fire witches?"

"Oh, they're not around any more. A lot of them died. Some were chased out of town. They went to Comonfort." Comonfort was a sleepy railroad-stop town some twenty miles from San Miguel. Chased to Comonfort like old Catskills comedians.

"Who chased them?"

"Priests," Carlos said, behind me. "There were three priests in town who wanted to get rid of them."

I turned and blinked at him. I looked for his eyes to crinkle but he just looked over my shoulder to his where his mother added cinnamon sticks to the pot.

"They were horrible, suffocating babies and stuff," said Juana, stirring. "So these priests prayed powerful prayers for many days, and the witches left San Miguel."

"They were evil," Carlos said.

"When you kids were little, my neighbor, Doña Amelia ran over, saying, 'Come see, the witches sucked my baby! I tried to hide him under the bed, but they got him.' He had *chupones* all around his neck. All black and blue." Juana touched her neck in a half-circle, an invisible necklace of bruises. "The child died. After another one of her kids died, she moved to Mexico City. But the witches never bothered us. That's how they are. They bother some people, and not others." Juana dumped half a bag of sugar into the pot. "Of course, I was careful. I hung scissors, open to the shape of the cross, over all the doorways." She shrugged as if to say, see how I took care of you. I looked at Carlos again, hoping he would throw me a sly look. But he only took a cup of sweet-smelling tea from his mother, blew on it and sipped.

"Of the three priests who chased the ball-of-fire witches, two have died," Carlos said. "I'm afraid of what will happen when the third dies."

I imagined my sister and her hedge fund genius from

D.C. in the kitchen. He be wearing his you're-kidding-me look. Some Catholics thought believing in ghosts put you in league with the devil. But I didn't feel like I was going to hell. Back when I had gone to that student party, Carlos had said there was going to be an earthquake. He had also said we were going to have a child together. I nudged him and we went downstairs, where we sat back into the lumpy pillows. I held the cup of tea in one hand and rubbed the hairless back of his wrist, where his hand lay on my leg, with the other.

"I've never been in my bed naked before," Carlos whispered an hour later. My overalls lay flung across a barbell made of chile cans filled with cement.

"You're kidding." I ran a finger up the hollow in his chest, slick from our sportsmanship. We lay silent, Carlos' ears tuned for Hugo's footsteps, and mine for ghosts.

"Move over here." We changed places so that I was next to the wall, Carlos' body shielding a view of my naked legs should the sheet slide away.

With the light out, the bedroom was completely black. I listened for wailing.

"Do you hear her?" I asked.

"Sometimes," my boyfriend said, pulling me close. I was jealous. I lay in a tiny single bed, listening for a deceased woman who wandered the house, trying to hear her so I could peek into the unnatural world. Believing in ghosts felt kind of spiritual, and perhaps with more spirituality, I would be better at Be Here Now. That way I could just stay in San Miguel and be OK with it.

I listened so hard I fell asleep.

I awoke alone, pulled my overalls on and stepped outside. The morning sun was startlingly high. Carlos grinned from the top of the steps.

"Carlos, there's something wrong with me. I can't wake up. I have to get to classes."

"You already missed one. *Ni modo.*" Doesn't matter.

Carlos placed a steaming plate of eggs, frijoles and tortillas in front of me and sat in the only other chair in the kitchen. The parakeets chirped from their cages on the wall over the patio sink. Outside, ranchero music blasted from a stereo speaker in an open window.

I gathered my books and hurried to school—a white girl on a dirt road in Mexico.

Girls in rubber sandals sauntered to the *tortilleria*, past little stores selling Bimbo bread and apple soda. Me with my big American haste. Hurrying was hard work. I felt like I was walking with ankle weights. As I turned toward the hill that led to the school, I was roused from my stupor by a tug on my elbow.

"Come on," Carlos said. He steered me to a downtown street and we ducked under a doorway that said *Laboratorio* overhead.

Waiting on a plastic chair, I gave in to my fatigue and dropped my head onto Carlos' shoulder. A man in a white lab coat handed Carlos a plastic cup.

"Bring the sample back first thing tomorrow."

"See," Carlos said when the lab guy disappeared. "You'll have to stay at my house again."

"Why?" I mumbled, eyes closed.

"To get your first-thing-in-the-morning sample, and because I never want you to go home."

With effort, I opened my eyes and walked into the blinding sun on my boyfriend's arm. Boyfriend. Isn't that what he was—as in temporary mate? Had he just said he didn't want me to leave? I stumbled along, out of downtown, back through Colonia San Antonio to the lamina-roofed house, wondering why I didn't feel more panic at the thought of never escaping.

I spent some more nights at Carlos' house, which let me see how he lived. It wasn't too complicated. School, basketball, shower, meal. Repeat.

Antibiotics had taken care of the energy-robbing intestinal parasites and I was back teaching classes. We were formal with each other in school, but after, I went with Carlos to the park, the store, wherever he was going. In the back of my mind I knew I was behaving like a lovesick Seventeen magazine subscriber. But I didn't care. Walking around the neighborhood with Carlos was enough for me.

One day we headed over to El Sexy's house to tell him about a basketball scrimmage in the park.

"Come in, *Doña*," said Carlos' friend's mother. She disappeared into the kitchen.

"*Doña*?" I giggled when she'd left the room. *Doña* was a term for older, distinguished, respected ladies.

"She thinks you're the bank president," Carlos said wryly.

"Only what I deserve," I whispered back, although I felt like an idiot—thirty-four years old now, making social plans with adolescents. That was when the thoughts I tried to keep away crowded in. *Going to the park with a bunch of teenagers wasn't a life.*

Jane had written that she couldn't wait for me any longer. She had another roommate living up on the third floor. My third floor. What had they done with my photos? The winter clothes I left in the closet?

I couldn't decide if I was mad about the new roommate on Tasker Street. The school director had been ducking me for five weeks. Every time I asked for my salary, he spread his hands, shrugged and smirked, reminding me with his look I was working illegally, there was nothing signed between us. Maybe I wanted the new girl out of my old room so I could move back.

But nights I snuggled next to Carlos' body. We didn't care if we were in my house or his; we needed our bodies melded warmly together. I sighed when he pushed the hair back from my face. I kissed his back when we spooned in the dark.

Maybe the new roommate was my sign to stay in Mexico a little longer.

LIGHTS IN THE CORNER

It was one week before Easter. Our Lord of the Column, a sacred statue that resided in the ancient church revered as a sanctuary in nearby Atotonilco, would be carried in an all-night procession to San Miguel, as it was every year during Holy Week. It would enter the city from Calle Independencia, and travel under flags, palm arches and white paper flowers that adorned my street. All day my neighbors had been out, on ladders and overturned buckets, hanging purple and white flags across the street.

Carlos and I slept at midnight, when the pilgrims were to have left the sacred church in Atotonilco. When a flat-toned song rose from the hills, we awoke and climbed to the roof. Dawn was edging aside the starry night. A column of people in house dresses and polyester sweaters and work pants and jackets appeared on the rise at the top of the street. Soon, the pilgrims were walking past our house, while we watched from the roof.

Women held sleeping babies next to their breasts in

rebozos. Men carried their hats in their hands. Some of the faithful held flowers. I marveled at their spirituality – or maybe it was the docility of blind followers—walking in the chilly hours of the night to honor Jesus.

I sighed enviously. I wanted to find comfort in the church, but the Catholic Church I grew up with honored virgins and said sex was for procreation only. When I was in eighth grade, I had to go to decency rallies in St. Dorothy's parking lot. We waved around placards that identified us as members of SUDS—Students for a Decent Society. A local DJ pledged not to play songs with profanity, and somebody drummed up support for picketing *Barbarella* at our neighborhood theatre. We were supposed to be against movies with nudity and songs with dirty lyrics and unwed mothers. Here I was something almost as bad – a girl in her thirties having out-of-wedlock sex.

Carlos had another view of religion. He was Catholic but didn't believe in Confession. He thought priests were only in it for the free housing. He made bargains with the Virgin of Guadalupe.

The life-sized statue of *El Senor de la Columna* floated past us below. Jesus' hands were tied to a column. His head was crowned with thorns and his wooden and plaster of Paris back was torn and bloody.

At St. Dorothy's, I had dressed in a white dress, white patent leather shoes and mantilla every spring and walked, singing, with my class, from the auditorium to the church in an all-school May procession. Twenty-five docile and un-selfish Marys with hands folded in prayer. An eighth grade girl got to wear a long satiny cape and sit on the altar on a throne representing Mary—the Catholic school version of a homecoming queen. By eighth grade I didn't want the honor and wasn't chosen. I wanted life's rewards, complete with newspaper headlines like my father got.

Daylight pushed its way across the sky behind rosy

banners of light as the last of the all-night walkers descended the hill. Carlos grabbed my hand and we ran down the stairs and into the street. We caught up with the pilgrims and walked under the palm frond arches and over crushed flowers in the street. Around us people were singing. I felt their faith. I wanted to feel the peace I saw on their faces.

Ahead of us, six men were relieving the statue's carriers, ducking a shoulder under the timber edges, while the other men fell away. We followed Jesus' bloody back through more flagged and flowered streets to the San Juan de Dios church.

El Senor de La Columna was placed by the altar, where he would reside until after Easter. Then he would be returned to Atotonilco, and this church, like every church in San Miguel, would again be dominated by the kindly Virgin of Guadalupe in her star-flecked mantle, with side altars for the Virgin de la Salud, the Virgin of San Juan de Los Lagos and other incarnations of Mary, the mother of God. The female revered. Maybe that's why I felt comfortable in Mexico.

Carlos and I squeezed into a back pew and knelt. He held my hand tightly and bowed his head. I lowered mine and felt a welling of gratitude in my chest. For what? Six A.M. bells tolled. Light fell into the church from a side window. A priest came out and began morning Mass.

"What are you praying for?" I whispered.

"For us," Carlos said. Now tears squeezed from the corners of my eyes.

Around us, people murmured the second half of the Our Father in Spanish. A pigeon fluttered in the rounded adobe brick and mortar ceiling above. Surrounded by Mexican women shushing babies and men raking their fingers through uncombed hair, I was moved to believe that I had something tangible, even wonderful, with the young man at my side. Maybe something blessed.

///

In late spring, the nights were warm. Carlos and I sat with Hugo on a Jardín bench. The Parroquia clock was aglow, the town quiet. Gussie saluted us from across the street, and then approached. "I want to hear genuine Mexican music. And I want to dance," she declared. The brothers exchanged a look.

"We'll take you to hear Mexican music," Carlos said. "Meet us here in the Jardín on Saturday night at eight. Come dressed up."

Saturday night, Gussie and I drank wine and zipped ourselves into dresses.

"Maybe I'll dance with a cute boy tonight," Gussie sighed. The Frenchman had gone traveling for a month. We left our glasses in the bedroom and headed for the Jardín.

The brothers were standing under a tree, looking too dressed to sit on a bird-stained bench. Carlos wore white jeans and a paisley shirt, Hugo, a leather jacket. Carlos smelled of apricot shampoo.

"So, where are we going?" I asked.

"You'll see." The brothers headed up Calle Correo and Gussie and I followed. Carlos fell back every block or so and put his arm around me, then dropped his arm and walked with his brother again, chatting about sports. Since he'd met me, Carlos spent less and less time with Hugo, so I didn't mind that he joined his brother.

Just when I thought it was impossible to ascend more, we turned right and continued uphill. We passed the Mirador, where Carlos had told me the story of his mother cutting another woman's face with a Coke bottle. The town blinked sleepily below.

"Yo, I'm wearing heels," I complained as we continued uphill. Finally a gravel parking lot—sparse with cars. Light was coming from inside two entrance doors and men in dress shirts smoked cigarettes on the porch.

The cavernous hall was lit like a K-Mart. About twenty long tables, arranged one after another like bar codes, lined each side of the room. Dressed-up people sat eating from plastic forks at the tables, while little boys in miniature suits and slicked back hair scampered between the tables. The brothers walked purposefully down the left side of the room and Gussie and I followed. Our dresses were correct but our blonde hair was attracting stares.

At the last table sat a woman in a shiny patterned dress next to a man in a graying moustache who absently patted her hand. Under the table, the woman had slipped her shoes off. Across, an elderly woman, her hair coiled in a bun at the back of her neck, held a hand-crocheted rebozo around her shoulders. Carlos pulled out the folding chair next to the elderly señora and I gratefully sat. Hugo and Gussie slid into seats next to the couple. We were not in the back of the room, I realized, but the front. A microphone stood in the aisle next to us. At the table across the aisle, a bride in satiny white and a groom with wavy gelled hair ate creamed spaghetti.

A bowl of ice appeared on the table in front of us, then four bottles of Coke, then a full bottle of Bacardi. A young boy brought a bowl of pickled jalapenos. I picked up one of several small brass vases with paper flowers that adorned the table. Fernando y Angelica, 16 agosto, 1993 was engraved on the side. In a year, they would have an anniversary. In a year, where would I be? Would Susan and Carlos ever be engraved on cheap bric-a-brac?

"Is Fernando a friend of yours?" I asked Carlos.

"No," he said, without expression.

"Angelica?"

"I don't know her."

"Who invited you?"

"Besides some kid in the back I play basketball with, I

don't know anyone here."

"We crashed?" I hissed. Carlos shrugged.

"Gussie, we crashed this wedding!" I whispered loudly as she broke a crusty roll in two.

"What?" Gussie looked from me to the Ortega brothers, who sat back, looking like they'd swallowed canaries. "Ha ha!" she laughed. "Awesome!"

The boys poured Cokes and Gussie opened the bottle of rum. Soon four Styrofoam plates piled high with chicken, frijoles and spaghetti in cream sauce were placed in front of us.

"Carlos, how did you know there would be a wedding here?"

"There's a wedding here every Saturday night. We'll leave before midnight. All the men are drunk by then and fights break out." His face looked mature, concerned about getting the women out before danger set in.

"Ladies and gentlemen," said a man in a tieless suit, taking the microphone. "Thank you for your esteemed presence here tonight as we celebrate the marriage of Fernando and Angelica."

"*Beso, beso, beso!*" cried the room. The *novios* kissed.

"Such beautiful young people, such a long life ahead. Let's wish them many years together!" the host said. "*A bailar!*"

A romantic ballad was started up. The novios giggled at each other, and then the bride gathered her skirt up, and stood. The man across the table from me looked into his wife's eyes, and then looked at me. "Thirty-nine years," he said. "Almost forty years we've been married."

"Isn't that right, mother-in-law?" he said to the señora next to me. The older lady nodded and waved absently, rhinestones sparkling in her ears. The man took the hand of his wife of forty years and held it elegantly at his chest as she slipped her shoes on and rose from her seat.

One couple just starting. One couple had made it forty years together. What did it take? My parents had been married thirty-five years. The longest I'd been with a boyfriend had been with Scott, the tortured medical student, in college. Mistake. After, there was the reporter who gave me a blown up and framed photo of himself for Christmas, and then I was just the Sunday bartender who watched couples come in for brunch.

A lively ranchero song played while ladies cleared our plates. Gussie tapped her fingers on the table.

"C'mon, don't you want to dance?" she said to Hugo, who'd barely said a word. Our table partner had not missed a dance with his wife. The brothers rose and we took the dance floor. Gussie's blonde hair swung like a flag from a different country.

Dancing always made me happy. I danced in late-night clubs in Philly to chase away my loneliness. I remembered dancing with Carlos at Laberintos on our first date, Hugo dancing with Gussie then too. I felt happy just then, light in my body. We swung through several more traditional tunes, foreheads gleaming, our table neighbor grinning at us.

Back at the table, Carlos poured four rum and Cokes into plastic cups. "Who's the Bee Gee?" Carlos asked. Out on the floor, a middle-aged dancer was clearing a path with swinging elbows. His shirt was unbuttoned past his solar plexus and two flaps of hair swept away from a middle part, wrapping around his head to fold over one another like wings in the back. The Bee Gees were from my time, my world. When I looked at Carlos curiously, he shot me a grin back. "Who's the Bee Gee?" I repeated, and laughed out loud.

Carlos stuck his hand under his shirt and scratched his chest as we walked home, which meant he was nervous. He let Hugo and Gussie go ahead as we descended a steep flight of zigzagging stone steps between two narrow streets. In front of a stone fountain, he stopped and took my wrist.

"My mother wants to know if you want to live in the house," Carlos said. An electric thrill shot through my body. In 34 years, I'd never been proposed to, nor been asked to live with a man. I felt like the first time I'd been asked out on a date, breathless and unbelieving.

Carlos wanted me to live with him. We'd have clothes in a drawer together. Toothbrushes side by side. No more running back and forth with a backpack stuffed with clothes.

Gussie wanted to move anyway, ever since her dog had scared away two boys climbing over our back wall one night while we slept.

Nobody in Carlos' neighborhood spoke English. My Spanish would improve and my accent would disappear. I would eat *huevos a la Mexicana* and chicken mole and give Juana money for food. All the girls in the neighborhood would know I was with Carlos.

It would be wonderful.

I thought of the bride and groom, of how, when they were eating, she had leaned into his shoulder and tenderly wiped his chin. I thought of the couple married forty years, and how the man had waited behind his wife's chair while she slipped her shoes back on, then took her hand and led her out to dance. It was heartbreakingly beautiful.

"What do *you* want?" I asked.

"I want you to live with me."

"Why?"

"Because I wake up thinking of you and go to sleep thinking of you. Because you appreciate the best parts of me in a way my family doesn't. Because you are a good influence on my life."

O.K. once we got his mother out of the way, he'd said

it. *I want you to live with me.* It was good enough for me. Part of me knew I was doomed, but a stronger part only wanted to be with Carlos. If he was in an overcrowded house with chickens scratching outside in the dirt, that's where I would be.

I had come to Mexico looking for solitude, and for time to write my book. I was giving that up now to gain something I thought I'd never have. Weeks before I'd set out for Mexico, I'd sat at a table at the White Dog Café, a glass of wine in front of me, crying into my folded arms. The last dinner had long been served. I'd closed my accounts and my tips were tucked deep into my pocket. The cooks were swabbing down the kitchen, playing a Jane's Addiction tape full blast.

Jane says, she's never been in love, no, don't know what it is, only knows when someone wants her. I want them if they want me. I only know they want me.

I lifted my head and sang along, wiping my nose. The refrain defined me. It played through my head when I was sliding plates into a bus pan, tying on my running shoes, drawing liquid black eyeliner across my eyelid. I'd heard it riding the bus from the Texas border.

Jane says, she's never been in love, no, don't know what it is, only knows when someone wants her.

I felt no uncertainty accepting the invitation to live in the lamina-roofed house. After years of searching for a worthwhile man to love, God had sent me someone. Why Mr. Right came disguised as a poor Mexican teenager, I did not question. "Jane Says" was gone from my head.

///

Juana clapped her hands together when I brought Gussie's chicken into the house along with my word processor, motorcycle boots and Indiana Pacers T-shirts. Gussie's yardless new apartment was unsuitable for livestock, and she'd given it to me.

"*Un caldo,*" Juana crowed. All of Juana's chickens had become caldo in previous weeks. Maximo was between construction jobs and the family was dining on frijoles three times a day.

"How's the chicken?" Gussie asked a few days later at the publicity office where we both did part time work.

"I think I got in good with Juana, moving in with a chicken. She's out buying vegetables to make soup."

Gussie's mouth dropped open. "Not my chicken!" Gussie's chair fell back with a clatter. I followed her out the door and into the street where men with pushcarts, women with babies, school children and Coca-Cola deliverers up on their truck stared as we streaked past.

"Where?" she gasped at the end of Calle Orizaba. I pointed and we ran to the mouth of the drainpipe, then down the rocky hill, leaping over discarded plastic Cloralex bottles.

The chicken was tied by the ankle to a kitchen chair. He clucked and pecked at the floor.

"Poor baby!" Gussie cried. She untied the string and gathered the chicken in her arms. Juana watched from the doorway of the laundry room, four steps above. Gussie held the chicken under an armpit and looked around. She took in the birdcages, the avocado stone and empty rice bag on the floor, the nails in the dirt of a planter, the kitchen chair with no back. Then she looked at me—with pity?

"Cool sink," Gussie said, pointing at the concrete pissing boy. "Ya me voy," she said to Juana. She carried the chicken out the door and I shrugged at Juana. Juana wiped her hands on her apron and smiled, confused and amused that a chicken deserved to live a long and happy life.

///

"Don't you see it?" Carlos asked me.

"What?" I whispered. It was the third night of living in

the house. We lay in bed, alone in the room. I was almost asleep but hearing the alarm in Carlos' voice, I became alert.

"I can't move."

"What's wrong?"

"There. Don't you see those lights in the corner?"

"I don't see anything."

"I think it's my grandfather."

"What do you mean? He was just here." Juana's father was a picture postcard Mexican man—huaraches, poncho, straw hat. He had visited earlier that week, sitting outside on the rocks, refusing to come in, so Juana had brought his bowl of frijoles and chopped chile and onion outside.

"No, my other grandfather who's been dead for about ten years. You don't see those lights blinking there?" Carlos shifted his eyes at me without turning his head.

I looked very hard at the dark corner. "I don't see a thing. What do you mean, your grandfather?"

"I feel his presence."

I looked around the room wildly, jealous. I wanted to see the lights.

"Carlos, you're scaring me."

"There." He began to twist his head, ever so slightly, side to side. "He left."

"Where'd he go?"

Carlos looked at me as if the question had never occurred to him.

"*Viene y se va.*"

"He comes and goes."

"Sí."

"Like my life," I laughed. "Here and gone."

"Don't say that."

"Oh, O.K." I had stopped asking myself the questions. But now I wondered. Would I be? Here and gone?

I LOVE LUCY

"She's the mother of my children," Eric Estrada told a friend in anguished tones on TV. He wore his black leather vest. Johnny still couldn't decide between his wife and his teenage girlfriend.

We lay on Carlos' single childhood bed that sagged in the middle. Hugo was at the park as usual. I punched my feather pillow to fluff it up. The wife, played by Laura León, a Mexican torch singer, had cascading blonde hair. "Carlos, everybody's white!" I said, flinging a hand at the television.

"*Así es,*" Carlos replied without expression. That's how it is.

"Nobody in this barrio looks like them." Everyone who lived in the casitas around the lamina-roofed house was like Carlos—brown as shoe leather. There were some guys with guns on the screen now and a white Mexican Mafioso, well past fifty, wearing a black shirt open to his pale, hairy middle.

"Don't you get mad that nobody on TV ever looks like you?" I asked, getting mad. Carlos shrugged and picked up a beef taco from the plate on the bed between us. While I read, Carlos had sautéed the onions, grilled the meat, heated the tacos and put the salsa in a bowl, as I liked it. It still didn't placate me. I grabbed *Labyrinth of Solitude* from the alcove behind us, annoyed, and noisily turned the pages. Octavio Paz said the Mexican male was resigned, patient, long-suffering, and does not reveal his interior.

"That wife has the biggest ass on television," I commented, glancing at Laura León.

"In a good way," Carlos said.

"That's what you like?" I asked incredulously. I had thin legs and a runner's ass—compact—or to put it another way—skinny.

"I like any figure on a woman, big or little, as long as all the parts are in their place."

Carlos, the middle child—the peacekeeper.

I understood more Spanish, but didn't feel like concentrating on the stupid racist soap.

"I thought you were reading that gringo who was in Mexico," Carlos said. I draped a leg over Carlos' leg to give him approval for noticing that I'd been reading Graham Greene. But I couldn't get past what was really annoying me—that Carlos didn't read.

I'd explored the entire house by now. It contained only one other room besides the kitchen and the downstairs bedroom. There were no books anywhere except on a shelf over the toilet in the doorless bathroom, where a third grade history book was perched. When the house ran out of toilet paper, pages with color pictures of the Aztecs, Quetzalcóatl and the eagle on the cactus disappeared.

When I was a kid my mother bought the World Book Encyclopedia from a door-to-door salesman for our homework projects. She took me to the children's section in the library every two weeks. Wouldn't it just take my mother seeing me in this house, in an exposed brick room occupied by a television and basketball shoes and the chile can and cement barbell, but no books, to make her start talking about Kevin O'Shea the golf pro?

I twisted away from my boyfriend. There was a white newscaster on the screen now, giving the news.

"Are newscasters here fair and impartial?" I asked in my looking-for-a-fight voice. "That's what I was taught in journalism school."

"Ha. This is the government's version of the news."

"How can you even watch it?" I asked disgustedly. I lowered my eyes to my book. Growing up, my sister and I had had matching twin beds, with identical bookshelves lined with Nancy Drew mysteries. Carlos didn't have a favorite childhood series. He didn't have a favorite book.

Carlos watched me reading then looked back at the blue glare of the black and white TV. I would try to find him a book. Carlos wasn't unintelligent. He knew more English than anyone in the school. When I spoke my language, he understood.

"Carlos, your brothers and sisters watched American cartoons when you were kids?"

"Sí."

"But they don't speak English."

Carlos laughed. "No, nada.

"You have a gift with language. With words."

"Listen, how you feel about words, that's how I feel about basketball, and painting."

I felt better, and dumber with my narrow view of what was smart. My sister was sending me gasping letters from Washington DC, asking what kind of intellectual life I could possibly have with a high-schooler. What she didn't get was that I was learning another language, and that when Carlos whispered that he loved me in Spanish, I felt like a fresh breeze blew across my soul.

I heard the front door squeak open, steps and then the kitchen's two metal chair legs scrape across the floor over our heads.

"My brothers," Carlos said, standing. "I'm going to go up and see, you know, how the night went." I kept my eyes on the book. Carlos jiggled my knee.

I shrugged and nodded. He wanted to know who played, who won, who argued with the refs. Men sitting around, talking about basketball, the women in another room. I knew *that* scene.

Carlos went upstairs. Minutes later, he stood at the bedroom doorway, scratching under his T-shirt.

"The boys are hungry," Carlos said.

"Are you going to make something to eat with them?"

"Nah."

"What's wrong?"

"Gerónimo wanted me to get you up to come make them something to eat." Carlos looked half-hopeful, half-apologetic.

"What?" I choked. On the radio, I'd listened to a ranchero classic in which the singer wails about how useless he is—he doesn't work or contribute to the family—but he continues being the king. It was sung without irony. Carlos' brothers were at the kitchen table, waiting for me to pad upstairs and fry eggs and frijoles while they sat like royalty, like some old episode of the Honeymooners. I could barely speak. "Carlos, what did you tell him?"

"I said I wouldn't ask you," he quickly replied. "Lupe would have done it, you see."

"Oh please," I said dully. "Don't tell me more."

Of course, Lupe would have done it. Lupe—who still carried a torch for Carlos' brother even though she was his ex. I *was* Lucy, wasn't I? The fair-haired girl with the handsome Latino—haplessly trying to make her way through a world she didn't understand. I wanted to get to the end of the half-hour, to where Mr. Guapo puts his arms around me and says, "Aw, Suzy," and I forget all the madness that has gone on before because now he is holding me close. That was why I was in a tiny brick house in a poor neighborhood, wasn't it? To sleep with my boyfriend every night, to live side by side. But he was upstairs again with his brothers, their laughter bouncing off the kitchen walls.

I threw the *ropa vieja* pillow on the floor, hoped Hugo tripped on it when he came in, turned off the light. I spread myself across the middle of Carlos' mattress, leaving no room. He would have to work to get into bed with me.

///

In the kitchen, days later, Lupe warmed tortillas. Gerónimo sat at one of the two chairs at the table with a plate of mashed frijoles. Lupe leaned her fleshy left breast against Gerónimo's arm as she spooned rice onto his plate. The older sister Mariana had been in the kitchen that week, bouncing her baby at her hip and stating that Gerónimo was the *mas guapo de la familia*, which made me laugh. Handsomest, my foot. *Gerónimo no era feo*, as they say. He wasn't ugly. Carlos had more beautiful, and kinder eyes. But, Gerónimo was lighter than Carlos and Hugo. Was that the key to looks in the barrio? And what kind of family talked like that anyway? Plus didn't anyone notice that now that he'd been going to bars at night and sleeping in the day, he was growing a tire around his middle. When he wasn't pissed off, like when Lupe got near him, Gerónimo had an amused look about him, an intellect in a world of buffoons, even though he had dropped out of high school.

Gerónimo swatted Lupe away like a housefly. She sat next to him and entwined her chubby calf around his chair leg. I stood at the boy-pissing sink outside the kitchen, making a long chore out of washing my hands, fascinated and repulsed by how Gerónimo sat with his head over his plate, ignoring Lupe, and how Lupe fluttered around, pushing the bowl of salsa closer, serving more frijoles, dropping warmed tortillas onto his plate. I remembered Gerónimo expecting me to go upstairs and make late-night eggs for the boys. Did the rest of the women in the house mind being servants? Or had they not figured out life offered other rewards besides the glance of a man shoveling food into his mouth?

"Carlos, do you think Lupe is going to live here forever?" I asked in our downstairs room.

"They're not married," Carlos told me.

"What? They've got two kids!"

"*No se,*" he said. "She's been here since she was 13 years old."

"How many girls have lived in this house?"

"You and Lupe, that's all," Carlos said. "Lupe and Gerónimo have broken up a million times."

"And gotten back together."

"Sí."

"So she still thinks she has a chance to get back with Gerónimo."

"I guess."

"Do you think they will?" Disbelief was written all over my face.

"God only knows. They're both crazy."

"So..." I couldn't let it rest. "But Gerónimo doesn't love her anymore."

"He has blackened her eye more than once. She has had him thrown in jail. It's been going on for about ten years."

"But they're still in the same house. Why does your mother let her stay?"

"Kids are neglected in Lupe's mother's house," Carlos said in a patient voice, as if he were explaining something to a child. "In fact, they threw her out when she was thirteen."

"How could that have happened?"

"Nobody could stand her."

That I could understand. She yelled at her kids constantly, and muttered about everybody behind their backs. I steered clear of her.

"Teenagers can be unbearable but you don't kick them out of the house." Now I was beginning to feel sorry for Lupe. I didn't want that. Disliking her was much less complicated.

"Why does your mother let Lupe stay?" I repeated.

Carlos looked at me as if I was dense. "The little boys," he said patiently, "are her grandchildren."

///

Dulce's bed against the far wall was lined with pink plastic yellow-haired baby dolls. Hugo slept six feet away from us in a single bed surrounded by a garden of dirty socks. Both came in at night late, after we were asleep.

Sorority girls I'd known in college had slept in "sleeping porches" of up to two-dozen beds, windows left open in Wisconsin winters so germs could find their way out. Co-ed dorms were common, too, on the Madison campus in the late seventies. So what was so weird about sleeping with your boyfriend and his brother and sister?

I sat cross-legged on the bed with notebooks in front of me one evening, preparing a lesson on personal pronouns when Dulce entered with a broom and piece of cardboard and began to sweep up Hugo's potato chip bags from the night before. She'd barely spoken two words to me since I had moved in, although she'd made a space for my word processor on a shelf made of a slat of wood on two piles of bricks. Dulce picked up her brothers' crumpled clothing from the floor without glancing at me. Would she talk to me if I helped her pick up crusty socks? Huh. Good thing

I was already occupied.

Dulce tossed the clothes pile outside the door. She knelt on her bed and began to peel a poster of an angelic looking child off the wall. A sentimental prayer was printed above the child's folded hands.

"What are you doing?" I asked.

"I'm going to put this over my father's bed to keep the ghost away," Dulce replied and went upstairs.

It was the first time she'd ever spoken to me directly.

I only felt comfortable in the house when Carlos was at my side. I went from the school to the lamina-roofed house every day and hardly saw Americans any more. I needed a friend. Maybe I would go with Dulce to fetch the atole in the morning.

For the boys who stayed in bed.

Not today, I thought. I'd rather walk on nails.

Scritch, scritch, scritch was the sound I woke to. Seven o'clock. Birds fed and plants watered, Juana began to sweep the kitchen floor over my head. "Dulce!" Juana yelled down the steps. Dulce heaved herself out of bed, slipped on rubber flip-flops and shuffled upstairs. Soon I heard water filling a bucket, and a mop slopping wetly onto the floor. Next, Dulce would wash the dishes and go over the hill with an empty soup pot to bring back steaming atole from Doña Lourdes. When the boys woke up, she would mash a panful of frijoles and scramble eggs with tomatoes and chiles.

I could never sleep past the sweeping hour. Once I heard the broom begin to scrape the concrete floor, I began to toss. I should be up there with the women helping. Were they rolling their eyes in contempt that I was still in bed? But I didn't want to get out of bed. There were the servers and the served. So far, I was served, which grouped me with the men for whom I had contempt for being so lazy. But heaven forbid I was going to be some tireless, unappreciated scrubwoman either.

It all made me mad. Only the women got up early. Lupe was at the washing sink shortly after 7:00 each morning, scrubbing clothes with a pink bar of Zote soap. Maximo was out of bed at 7:28 and at the kitchen table by 7:30, downing his frijoles with a crusty roll before he pedaled off to his construction job. Carlos and Hugo stayed in bed until they felt like getting up. When they went upstairs, they sat at the kitchen table or on the steps until Juana or Dulce gave them plates of hot food. Gerónimo never got out of bed before noon. From the downstairs room, I heard Lupe turn over a T-shirt with a wet slap.

I lay in bed, snuggled warmly next to Carlos. His arm pulled me back when I tried to get up. The broom scolded, scritch, scritch, scritch. I sat up, grabbed my terry cloth robe and padded to the shower room, passing Juana in the kitchen, who smiled at me but did not ask me to separate dry frijoles or wash dishes even though I slowed down to give her the chance.

Light entered the shower room through a skylight made of plastic sheeting and chicken wire. I moved the clog of hair and soap wrappings from the drain and kicked one of the old socks used for washcloths to the corner.

The house had no water heater, so I braced myself then turned the water on. I soaped body parts and rinsed myself off under the chilling spray.

I left some money on top of a bag of frijoles before I left for classes, even though I gave Juana money every Friday. "*Para comida*," I told her. I gave her food money to buy myself the right to stay in bed the following day.

///

Cuca lived in a dirt floor shack in Las Cuevitas, the slum that started at the bottom of the hill, meters away from the lamina-roofed house. The town's smelly brown arroyo snaked through the neighborhood.

Cuca had a wrinkled brown face. She kept her eyes down, but when spoken to, tilted her head up and blinked, looking off in the distance. She responded to requests to do things, like sweep, but not to questions about herself. Juana found her when she went out to water the garden under her kitchen window one morning, standing by the door.

Cuca's sister had died and Cuca was alone. The sister had worked as a maid and earned enough to feed them both, but now Cuca was eating tortillas and salt. Cuca, although she had never worked, thought maybe she could do some chores for food or money.

"I'll pay her to wash our clothes," I offered. Juana asked if she would wash the brothers' clothes too. So Cuca came just past eight and stood at the concrete sink most of the day, taking on the entire family's laundry. She sat on the step when she rested, and ate the bowl of frijoles topped with chopped tomato and ranchero cheese Juana gave her.

One day she whispered to Juana that they said the sister's house had not really belonged to the sister, and they were making her leave.

"How? Who said?" Juana asked indignantly. But Cuca tilted her head sideways and looked at something far away. The next day Cuca arrived with two blankets. After dark, Cuca put her blankets on the floor by the wash sink and slept between them.

Cuca scrubbed the clothes and the dishes, and made herself as small as possible when she rested on the step. She ate huge bowls of food, and I thought perhaps she would fatten up. One night, she began to sing.

Early the next morning, Hugo crashed into our downstairs room and threw himself onto his bed, pulling a wool blanket up over his head. Shortly after I'd moved in, Hugo had begun sleeping in the upstairs room, along with Gerónimo, Lupe and their two boys and Juana. Dulce was in León visiting cousins. "*Pinche vieja canta toda la noche*," he muttered. "*Y baila, la pinche loca.*" The dang lady sings all night long. And dances—the damn crazy lady.

"She sounds like Cher, don't you think?" Carlos asked.

Hugo and Gerónimo told their mother that a mentally ill person who sang and danced in battered high-heeled shoes all night long shouldn't be living in their house.

"But I can't just throw her out. She has nowhere to go," Juana said.

Cuca, for all her nocturnal performing, worked steadily through the day.

"Move the lovebirds upstairs with everybody else, and let the loca sleep downstairs where nobody has to listen to her," Gerónimo said.

Move us upstairs with the entire herd?! Get out of the entire crazy house is what I should do. I began checking ads for a downtown rental. Everything was way too expensive. I went to the roof and flung pebbles at the cactuses below.

Cuca was hanging clothes on the branches of the huizache tree outside the house one morning, when a man on a burro rode up the hill and took off his hat to her with a flourish. The next day he came again and began to sing. On the third day, Cuca took her blanket outside, spread it on the ground, and sat, arranging her legs to the side like a schoolgirl. She sang with the man. By the end of the week, they were married.

Cuca picked up her blankets, turned her back on our laundry and mounted the señor's burro.

"I'm going to miss the free entertainment," Carlos said as Cuca rode away. I didn't laugh. My boyfriend rubbed my shoulders, where they hunched into angry knots.

The room was pitch black, and Carlos and I stared into the darkness from our pillows, talking about how we'd spent Sundays as kids.

"Your brothers wore ties?!" Carlos asked.

"Of course," I giggled. "With their hair slicked back with VO5. And my sister and I wore dresses and patent leather Mary Jane's."

"I didn't go to church. I ate bananas and watched All Star Wrestling. Went out and played soccer with all my brothers including Martín."

"There's another brother?"

"My father's son. His mother is the one my mother sent to the hospital. Good soccer player. He comes around. You'll see him sooner or later. My mother thinks he only comes when he wants something from my father, but it's not true. He doesn't have other brothers or sisters. He comes when he misses us."

"Any more of you I don't know about?"

"I told you there's my brother Chepe who's in the States."

Right. Living in a trailer up the highway from affluent Naples where my parents wintered. He *owns* his trailer, Juana once proudly told me.

"And my mother has a son from before she was with my father. He's in León."

"Is that *it*?"

"That's all I know about."

I thought about it. I had nothing to say.

"I've never worn a tie."

"Don't sound so thrilled about it. Maybe you will at your high school graduation," I said encouragingly. "Don't you think you ought to go back and finish?"

The door opened, Hugo entered, and the bed creaked with his weight.

"Pinche Mama Mia's, hombre."

"You got in?" Carlos asked his brother, who was still seventeen.

"Pinche Alberto was at the door."

Carlos sucked in his breath.

"Place was filled with gringas. Short skirts, man. Every naco in town was hitting on them. So I ask for a Coke. The waiter brings me a rum and Coke and charges me thirty pesos, *pinche vago.*" Lame-ass bum.

Carlos shifted in the bed beside me.

"This girl's looking at me. Long legs. You wouldn't believe it. Red hair to her neck. An ass on her, man. Guys sniffing around her like dogs, and she's looking at *me.*"

Carlos coughed. "*Me dices despues, no?*" Tell me later.

I rolled onto my side. Why hadn't I known when I was nineteen that men were like this? Hugo fell silent. I pressed myself into Carlos' back, the only place I felt safe.

TWO RED LINES

I loved my motorcycle boots, the ones I'd worn on my first date with Carlos. They were sold to me by a guy with a scarlet mohawk at a shop on South Street in Philly where dresses with holes cut out of them hung from motorcycle handlebars and shoes were displayed in cages. They'd cost a hundred and twenty-five dollars, had square toes, buckles on the sides, and cloth pull-on tabs. Now I couldn't find them anywhere. Which didn't make sense because they didn't fit anyone besides me.

"My motorcycle boots?" I asked Carlos, peering under the bed again. He looked alarmed, and then dashed out the door. I followed.

Outside the house, below on the rocky dirt road the trash truck was pulling away preceded by a boy who beat a metal rod with a metal stick – clang, clang, clang – to tell residents to bring their trash down.

Inside, in the upstairs room, Juana finished arranging shoes in a row and wiped her hands on her skirt. "Ya, ev-

erything fits better now that I got rid of that *chanclero*."
That pile-up of shoes. "I cleared all the old shoes out of the
alcove under the stairs too."

Carlos looked at me sympathetically. We went outside,
sat on some rocks. I heard the trash truck heading back to
the Ancha, its clang, clang, clang growing distant.

My hip, short bleached hair had grown out, and my
motorcycle boots were gone. I stood on a rock with my
arms folded and glared at the neighborhood for awhile,
then sat and leaned into Carlos, who tugged the ends of
my brown and straw-colored hair to cheer me up. Maybe
I didn't need the boots, the tough look. No place to stomp
around out here in the barrio besides the rocky path leading to the house of the señora who sold atole. We hadn't
been to a disco in months.

The elote guy came by with his plastic bucket. Carlos
dug in his pocket for change and bought us two cobs of
corn. The guy rubbed them with lime then sprinkled them
with chile and salt, and we sat on the rocks and ate them.

I remained calm and forgiving for a couple of days.
Then I couldn't find my genuine Levis that were getting
thin in the knees. I checked the pile of dirty clothes I dis-
creetly kept under Carlos' bed. I intended to learn to wash
my clothes by hand when nobody was looking. The jeans
weren't there and neither were a lot of my T-shirts or underwear.

Snooping, I found my sweatshirt upstairs on the top of
a geranium in an aluminum planter but there was no sign
of anything else.

Then one morning my Indiana Pacers T-shirt appeared
on Maximo, along with a baseball cap I'd just bought at
an outdoor market, as he pedaled off to work. My favorite white T-shirt that I'd liberated from my father's drawer
before I left for Mexico showed up on Hugo, and early
one cool morning I found Dulce scraping fideo noodles

from a pot with a stone wearing my St. Joseph University sweatshirt.

The following day, I waited until Dulce went to the tortilleria. Juana was outside watering plants. I pulled clothes out of the three alcoves in the upstairs room wall and let them pile up on the floor. Out came Dulce's skirts, Carlos' jeans, Juana's blouses, an enormous bra. This solved the mystery of where clothes were kept. The wardrobe of nine people was in three wall alcoves. I rescued several shirts, my jeans, a ball of bikini underpants that looked as if it had been embarrassedly shoved to the back corner. I ran downstairs like a thief, folded my clothes carefully and stuck them in a Nike bag my father had given me.

"Carlos, where's my wool sweater?" I asked one chilly night. It was heavy cabled wool, purchased in Wisconsin about ten years prior with two entire nights' bar tips.

"I don't know," he shrugged.

I pawed through my clothes again and did an under-bed sweep. Upstairs, I rummaged through the family alcoves. "Looking for my wool sweater," I explained to Juana who was sitting on her bed, watching a telenovela. I investigated the shower room, climbed to the roof to check the clothesline and searched the tops of birdcages.

Downstairs I stood in front of the television screen and faced my boyfriend. "It's my best sweater and it has disappeared. Everyone takes my T-shirts and never asks. I buy all the deodorant, body lotion and hairspray in the house and everybody uses them and never replaces them!" I said, my voice rising. "I don't get any respect around here. It's *my* sweater and it's gone!" I almost stomped my foot.

Carlos' eyes said he hoped his brothers wouldn't come into the room and see his insane girlfriend losing it over a sweater.

"That's it," I cried, while Carlos craned his head to see his soccer game on TV. I grabbed my giant box of tampons, which Mexican women did not use, much less leave in sight, from its hiding place under my socks and slammed it down in front of my clothes. I grabbed my jeans jacket, which hadn't been carried off because it was too small to fit anyone, I was sure. I stormed out of the house and sat on the stone ledge up the hill. I felt like walking into town and finding a bar. Then I remembered going into San Miguel bars the summer before I met Carlos. American and Mexican men with their hot breath too close, arm over the back of my seat, breaking their arms to flag down the bartender to give me a cuba I didn't want. I felt trapped. I hated the starry sky above me.

I pretended I didn't see Carlos walking up the hill toward me. He sat down on the ledge and opened his hand to offer something—a package of gum. I had a twenty-year old boyfriend who tried to charm me with gum. I took it and stuffed it in my pocket.

I sighed. Carlos owned a decent pair of basketball shoes and a backpack. Hugo wore the same basketball shoes to practice six days a week, and sometimes I saw them pedal off on their father's feet in place of construction boots. Carlos didn't seem to resent it, which made me feel petty.

Still. Gum!

"Gerónimo tried your sweater on. I got it back for you."

"Carlos, my stuff is MINE!" Now I felt twelve again, almost at foot-stomping.

Carlos waited for me to calm down. "Gerónimo, as the oldest son, was very spoiled when we were young. He got used to having the best of everything. When my father brought clothing home from D.F., Gerónimo got the first pick. My mother always served him first at meal time."

"That's not fair. How could you stand it?"

"My parents got together and started having their children when they were teens. My father's family didn't like my mother because she was his second woman. My parents worked out their jealousies through lots of fighting; sometimes things got thrown and people were hit. As the oldest, Gerónimo bore the brunt of their violent years. Spoiling him was a way of making up for it. I guess they didn't do him any favors."

More evidence that Juana was hellfire. And Carlos had just managed to make me feel sorry for and not quite mad at Gerónimo anymore.

"Don't you get pissed off you don't own your own shoes?"

"It's always been this way," Carlos said. What if I married him, and he expected that one pair of shoes between several kids was enough?

"I don't want your brothers taking my things and I need your support."

"OK." Now he was wearing his amused look.

"I mean it!"

"I know."

I remembered going to the Ring, and Carlos fending off men with glares, and the relief I felt. I got off my rock, went over, hugged my arms around his shoulders. "Don't you want to own your own shoes and have nobody touch them?"

"Sí. I can think of other things I want more."

"Like what?"

Carlos didn't say anything for a long moment. "Like college."

"Say it again!"

"No."

"Say it!"

He just looked at me as if I were an amusing circus act.

"You said it. I heard you!" I punched his shoulder to let him know I would never forget this, never ever.

Maybe I represented a way out of this life. This was good. I could only do so much adjusting. I wanted out of this life too.

///

It was nine at night, and I was buying milk in the store up the hill from the house. Kids playing the video machine next to the Coke bottles stared at me while I took my change. Outside Dulce sat on the stone ledge between the top of the hill, gossiping with Luisa, who lived at the bottom, and who was pregnant again but, like with her first two, wouldn't say who the father was. Dulce and Luisa sat side-by-side swinging their legs, their T-shirts still wet in a band across their waists from leaning over sinks washing dishes.

I wondered where Dulce spent her nighttime hours. She usually didn't come back into the house until after we were asleep. Lupe had gotten mad at somebody and left with her boys again, and Hugo slept in her bed upstairs.

"How come Dulce stays out at night?" I asked Carlos.

"She and my mother aren't speaking. Something about food."

Maximo was between construction jobs and Juana had gotten a job cooking in a restaurant. She left Dulce money to make comida every day. "*Caldo de pollo*," Juana ordered on Monday, but Dulce made frijoles and *chicharón*. "*Bifstek con cebolla y chile*," Juana said on Tuesday and Dulce made *milanesas de pollo*.

I was sorry the women of the house were fighting, but not really because but it meant Carlos and I were gloriously alone. We snuggled and watched TV. We made love as if any minute our freedom would end. We were not wrong.

Saturday afternoon, Mariana's oldest, Alicia, came. She helped Juana make a comida of meatballs and rice, and by dark was drinking lemongrass tea in the kitchen. By nine-thirty, she had cozied herself into Hugo's bed next to us. Clearly, she meant to spend the night. I was reading a book. I turned on my side, giving her my back. How could these people live without privacy? I had to get out of this house, and take my boyfriend with me.

///

Dulce ran into the house, shouting "Eva's coming! Eva's coming!" She dropped the kilo of warm tortillas wrapped in her mother's embroidered cloth on the kitchen table.

"Our cousin from León," she told me breathlessly as she ran past.

I stood at the metal door.

Walking up the path from below was a tiny, pretty woman not much older than twenty. In her arms she held a baby, and behind her trailed three small children. Eva wore a black dance skirt with a sheen the sun bounced off, a polyester sweater and dusty patent leather high heels. When Dulce reached her, she took the baby boy from Eva's arms and snuggled it on her right hip.

"Ma!" Dulce shouted into the house. "Eva's here!" Juana appeared at the top of the stairs to the upper room. "Eva," she said with a tight mouth, as her niece stood in the entrance, smiling. "Have you eaten?"

Juana wrung out the pants she was washing at the *pila*, the wash sink. She took down a bag of rice and went into the kitchen.

I thought I'd be helpful and take a suitcase, but there was none. There was not a backpack, nor a diaper bag in any hand that passed through the door, although the baby looked to be about a year old. The two hiding behind Eva's skirt were solemn-faced boys in T-shirts and miniature elastic-waisted men's pants. Holding the boys' hands was a girl of about six. She wore a flowered dress and a worried expression. They stood in the tiny patio and looked around.

Just as I decided to hide from the crowd in our down-stairs room, Dulce descended from the roof with a five-foot high roll of foam padding. Eva and the children stood motionless in the doorway like a painting.

"You'll all fit on this," Dulce said, unrolling the foam on the floor to demonstrate. It took all the floor space between the beds. They weren't going to get on an afternoon bus and return to León. The baby started to cry.

Eva had had a fight with her husband, threatened to go live with her Tia Juana and made good. The boys were all hers—Eva was 23 it turned out—and the girl whom they called Reynita was her little sister. In León, she spent the day caring for the four children.

"I'm never going back to that good-for-nothing," Eva proclaimed three days later. She made herself useful sweeping the front step. She polished the bathroom mirror with newspaper, washed out her sweater, and accompanied Dulce up the hill for tortillas, a dust cloud of kids following. Juana made huge pots of frijoles and bought an extra kilo of tortillas every day. "I can't continue to feed all these kids," she grumbled when Eva wasn't around. "I can only stretch my food budget so far. Now Eva says the boys need milk. Where am I going to get money for milk?"

I was modeling in many art classes. I had milk money but I didn't want Eva and her kids to stay, sniffing and whimpering in the night inches away from where I slept with Carlos, spooned into one another in descending order like a big fat comma. Instead of diapers, the baby was wrapped in fuzzy strips of an old blanket that were washed every other day. The sad, quiet oldest boy began to defecate in his pants and on the floor. They needed more than milk to make them better.

The babies cried at night when Eva went out with Gerónimo. Eva polished her patent leather shoes, brushed off her skirt and left the house with her cousin around nine, bound for the discos, for a nighttime freedom she had never experienced. She did not ask for babysitting favors. The children were simply left behind with Juana. The older boy pooped and Juana spent the night with a bucket and a bottle of Cloralex, cleaning up after him.

I rented a space in my friend Claudia's house as a writing studio, and moved my word processor and wooden table there. I sat in her clean room, and soaked up the silence. This used to be my life. I could have this again. But could I have silence, peace and organization and still have Carlos?

Carlos and I didn't eat donuts in bed and watch TV any more. We sat outside the house on rocks or walked the streets instead. I lost my appetite, having no place to sit down to eat. I wanted to not feel like a crazy, selfish person for wanting back what tiny amount of space and privacy we had claimed in the house. Just when I thought I would accidentally on-purpose step on Eva when I got out of our bed in the morning, Eva and the kids moved up to Juana and Maximo's room and Hugo moved back downstairs with us.

"Why doesn't your mother tell them to go home?" I asked Carlos. Growing up, I'd stayed at aunts' and uncles' houses, but my parents always called ahead, asked if the schedule was clear, made arrangements, then sent us with clothes, pillows and money for popsicles.

"Dulce stays at Eva's mother's house when she goes to León. Remember, she was just there for two months?"

"So Eva might stay two months?"

Carlos shrugged and picked up his basketball.

Eva got a job as a maid and began to buy disposable diapers. Then her husband appeared one morning, a thin guy with overlapping teeth, twisting his baseball cap in his hands at the doorway as I passed in my terry cloth robe, the towel I kept hidden downstairs wrapped around my head.

He was tall with thick black hair like the baby's, his frame stooped over as he stared at the step, my unlikely salvation. Take them away, I prayed silently.

Eva went outside while the children huddled on the concrete stairs. Voices rose. "Too long," I heard, and "new life." The door slammed and Eva's high heels clicked inside. Eva and Dulce climbed to the roof and watched Eva's husband's forlorn shoulders grow smaller as he descended from the house, until they disappeared into the trees that lined the arroyo.

I went to my rented room, and sat in a rage. I couldn't write. Move my whole self out next. That was the logical step—a room, a bed, a desk. Carlos could come stay with me again. But how would Juana feed all those people without the money I brought home from my job? Maximo was working but his salary covered bills and left only so much more for food. Why didn't I forget the whole crazy thing and go back to a sane existence in Philadelphia? My life had been fine. I would leave Carlos one day and return to it, hadn't that been my plan?

"I guess I better go back," Eva said the next day. By afternoon she and the babies were gone. The foam rubber pad was rolled and stashed on the roof again. Dulce went out at dusk in her rubber sandals and climbed to the top of the hill where her friend Luisa sat now with an infant in her arms. Carlos brought down a little table and set up some paints. I opened a book. I tried to savor every minute of peace. By now, I knew it could end at any minute.

TWO RED LINES

The Guns and Roses song blasting from the speaker in El Sexy's small bedroom was so loud it made conversation impossible, so Carlos and I went out on the second floor balcony to watch fireworks explode in the night. It was the last weekend of September and San Miguel was preparing to stage the 4 a.m. battle of St. Michael the Archangel and the devil once again. Hugo was back in school, but Carlos wasn't. He didn't have tuition money.

El Sexy came around offering Sabritas potato chips from the bag. Short, baby-faced Gabriel leaned on the stone wall next to us. I moved over to give him room and knocked a plastic cup half-filled with Coke to the street below.

Ha ha ha! From inside El Sexy's bedroom, Hugo's laugh boomed off the walls. He threw looks indicating he had just witnessed the stupidest act he had ever seen. His laughter subsided into prolonged snickers. I looked at Carlos and shook my head. Hugo wouldn't come out to the balcony because we were on it. Hugo and I hadn't spoken since I told him I thought it was rude to have taken my good leather belt without asking and to have punched an extra hole in it.

A tinny band started up below in the Jardín, playing a lively, chase-your-troubles-away tune, the sound of Mexican fiestas. I closed the balcony door to hear it without competition from Bon Jovi blasting from the speakers. Suddenly the door was pushed open so hard it swung out and crashed against the brick wall. Hugo stood glaring on the other side. Then he turned his back on me, disgust written on his face.

I ran down an outside flight of stone steps and stood under El Sexy's balcony, crying helpless tears.

"I don't belong," I cried to Carlos, who had followed me. "He despises me and I have to live in the same room as him. I never know what I'm doing wrong until it's too late."

There at the edge of the cobblestoned street was the plastic cup I'd knocked off the ledge. A balloon of anger rose in me then burst, leaving me exhausted and desolate.

"I don't know the rules. I don't know how to behave here. I'm a jerk because I don't want everyone to walk off with all my clothes. And my bike!"

I had saved up 400 pesos and bought a used bicycle with an American flag on the crossbar. I used it once, left it in the house in a small hallway that led to a cracked ceramic tile bathtub that nobody used. I saw my bicycle the next afternoon, whizzing down the Ancha de San Antonio, Hugo at the handlebars. Another day I saw El Sexy steering the bike up Calle Umaran, and a few days later Maximo rode it towards the outskirts of town, his homemade saw sticking out of the nylon knapsack on his back. Carlos held my shoulder.

"I can't exist between two cultures anymore," I sobbed.

"I'm supposed to do all the adapting. But nobody under-stands me. And nobody tries to. I want to go back to Phila-delphia."

He stiffened. "All this togetherness is a little too much?"

"It's just, I can't be *me* in your house."

Carlos crumbled a piece of stone wall with his finger. "You're going to leave?" Sometimes I thought I would, but now, spoken out loud, it sounded like a dirty secret. It sounded untrue.

"No, I didn't say that. I need you to listen to me, that's all."

I wiped one side of my face with the back of my hand. "I don't like how the men in your house are kings and the women are slaves. I'll go along with it when I'm in your house, but what am I going to teach my daughters?"

"You'll teach our daughters your ways."

"When are we going to have our kids?" I asked alertly.

"When we have money." Carlos looked fully at me.

"When's that going to be?" I held my breath, realizing in that very moment that I must be living in a cramped, ugly house for some reason, and that the reason was to have a future with Carlos.

"When I get a job."

"Bueno," I said excitedly. I forgot about Hugo and his teenage anger. I felt a warming around my heart, a swing back toward the how-can-I-ever-leave-him feeling.

"Yeah, I know I've got to work." Carlos had gotten his hair cut; it came to the top of his ears now. He looked older.

I threw my arms around his neck. "I get crazy when we just go along day after day without a plan. Carlos, you've got to work and you've got to finish high school."

"I'll work and save money then go back and finish school."

"That's a plan!" I hugged him. I felt like I could trust him. "Let's go dance in the Jardín."

"Let's go home and make fireworks instead."

///

A couple of weeks later, I woke before seven and bounded out of the house in my running shoes, full of awe at the pink morning. I ran down the hill to the path where a señora in a straw hat shooed goats with a stick. I crossed a large dusty cactus field and emerged at a lot on the highway where the Americans were lobbying to have a hospital built. A truck piled high with broccoli beeped at me as I jogged in place. Across the highway I crashed through brush and followed a dirt path overhung with low trees whose roots crept into the arroyo below. I rounded the back of a large hill as the sun lit the sky a cheery wake-up yellow. I climbed the hill, finding footholds, filling my lungs deeply, and life seemed worthwhile and good. At the top was a concrete cross, twice my height. I put my hands on my knees and watched sweat from my hairline drop onto the cement. At the base was a tin of fresh flowers, reminding me of faith.

Back in the room it was dark and cool. Hugo was sleeping in the upstairs room again. Carlos was alone. He slept as if his body was still curled around me. I wiped sweat from my face with the bottom of my T-shirt and leaned over him.

"Do you want coffee or babies?" I asked.

He stirred and rolled over slightly, arm at his forehead. "Babies," he said.

We sat on a Jardín bench a few nights later while night deepened from gray to black. Mariachis were playing under the portales, trying to drum up interest in being hired for weddings and parties.

"Carlos, it's autumn! My mother came to visit one year ago already." A year ago I'd been teaching school, a valid reason to stay in Mexico. Now I was modeling, translating, writing, bartending, helping my boyfriend save money to finish high school. Beyond graduation, Carlos didn't know what he wanted to do. We drifted along like the slow traffic on the Ancha and it was making me crazy. I needed plans, a future filled with promise.

I began to cry. My stomach had been upset for days, and I was tired. Maybe one more round of antibiotics for amoebas? But it was more than that. Hugo still wasn't talking to me and Carlos and I hadn't mentioned having kids since the night of the Alborada. Pretty soon, I was bawling, face in my hands.

"Let's get out of here," Carlos said tersely. He took my elbow and hustled me off the bench.

Carlos steered us quickly down Calle Umaran, looking for a quiet place to stash me until I finished my scene. We turned down Calle Jesus, where the doorways were darkened and quiet.

"Why do you have to cry in public?" Carlos said, his face tense.

"Women cry sometimes, that's all," I said defensively.

"People are going to think I hit you."

"What are you talking about?" I was shocked.

"Just stop crying. I don't want people to think I'm mistreating you."

Why were we talking about spouse beating? Gerónimo had hit Lupe in the past. And Carlos had hinted at violence between Máximo and kindly Juana. How could I think about living in Mexico? Well, men hit women in the United States too. I cried harder. Then I thought of going back to Philadelphia—bartending and going home alone at 3 A.M. again, putting my key in the lock with dread rumbling in my belly, looking over my shoulder and turning around completely once to let would-be attackers know they'd have to jump me head on. I leaned against a mesquite door and hiccupped. My shoulders heaved. In the dark of the deep doorway, Carlos pulled my head against his chest.

"Ya, ya, ya," he said. "What is it?"

"I don't know," I said, slumping against him. "Everything."

Two weeks later, I was proofreading a tourist guide in a downtown office, one of my jobs. We were on deadline; it was after ten. The director, an American woman named Lucy, ordered French fries and beer.

"Those potatoes were greasy," I complained. "I feel sick."

"Maybe you're pregnant," Lucy joked, removing the slick plate.

The words of a hotel ad floated in front of me. I stood up. Everything went out of focus; I sat down again. The smile faded from Lucy's face.

"I have a home pregnancy test," she said. "I'll bring it in tomorrow."

It was simple enough. I peed on a plastic wand the size of a Popsicle stick, put it down gingerly as if it was dynamite, and washed my hands. Gussie was in Lucy's office bathroom with me. The wand rested in an empty kitchen bowl. We watched for two pink lines to appear, indicating I was pregnant, or for nothing to happen on the chemical strip at all. We crouched next to the toilet with the bowl on the floor between us. I'd spent about fifteen years trying not to be pregnant. Now, suddenly, as I held the bathtub edge with trembling hand, I felt myself, oddly, deeply wishing for the lines to appear.

Gussie saw them first and gasped. Two faint pink lines. Was this why I cried in the Jardín and fell asleep at eight at night? Was this why my coffee suddenly had a bitter taste? The slashes on the wet paper went from pale to bold—two red lines pointing my life in a new direction.

"What are you going to do?" Gussie whispered,

alarmed, and then stopped short. I was smiling—a dazed, unbelieving, cartoonish grin. I was shocked to feel a profound joy moving through me. The answer to everything was there in my belly. I would not go back to Philadelphia and find a sensible man. I felt no regret, no hesitation, only joy, relief, resolution. I had my plan. I was thirty-four years old. I would stay in Mexico with Carlos and have a baby.

///

Sunday afternoon, the day's heat beat down on the lamina roof over our heads. Juana and Maximo sat on the edge of their bed in the upstairs room, stupefied in front of an old movie. Juana fanned herself with the water bill. We leaned against an old console stereo on which Maximo still spun early Rolling Stones and Elvis Presley albums. I was seven weeks along, sleeping in the afternoon. Had Juana noticed, or did she just figure everyone slept in the heat? I pinched Carlos' leg.

"Ma, Susana's going to have a baby," Carlos said.

"Susana," Juana said. She stopped fanning and looked me over slowly. "I'm going to squeeze you orange juice every morning. Make sure you drink it." Then she smiled at me, and I felt her approval. Not too many Mexican women had reached my age without having produced children.

"Why so nervous?" I asked in the kitchen as we helped ourselves to frijoles from the pot on the stove. Carlos flipped tortillas over in the gas flame with his fingers then shook his hand out. I uncovered the salsa—roasted tomatoes and green chiles—still in the *molcajete* where it was ground. A sharp flavor flew up my nose and I thought I might vomit.

"I don't want to be another Gerónimo," Carlos said.

Gerónimo had recently fathered a baby girl with another woman, the recent birth of which had provoked Lupe's flight with her two boys from Juana's house again. Both girlfriends and their children lived in their own mother's houses. Gerónimo didn't work.

"You're not like Gerónimo," I reminded my boyfriend fiercely. "That's why you're with me."

Carlos tapped my still-flat stomach gingerly. "These are amazing," he said, marveling at my round, blue-veined breasts. I searched for a curve in the flat-faced moon of my belly, lying on a patchwork quilt Gussie's grandmother had sewn over several bitter Maine winters. Gussie was up in Texas looking for buyers for the artesania she produced.

Minding Gussie's small apartment, we had a bathroom with a door, a little kitchen, a one-cup coffeemaker and an electric frying pan. I woke to chirping birds instead of Juana sweeping. I imagined us in the near future on a bed like this, on a homemade quilt, bouncing a cooing bundle between us. We were gloriously alone. We snuggled in bed. We made coffee in Gussie's percolator.

"What's this?" Carlos said, after sex our second day there. The tip of his penis was covered with a glistening smear of red.

"Maybe it's nothing," I said, but I was crying by the time I called the midwife I'd seen only once, because I knew that blood from a pregnant woman was the opposite of nothing; it was the last thing you wanted to see.

IN THE LOCKER ROOM

"Why don't we rent a little place?" I suggested a week later, back in our shared room in Carlos' parents' house. We lay on opposite beds, staring at each other. Carlos looked at me as if I was crazy.

"We have a place here," he said. We had half a bed, a third of a room and no privacy. I felt betrayed.

"I can't go on like this," I told Carlos. "This room already has four people in it. What if I get pregnant again? Where will we put one more?"

"We'll build a room," Carlos offered.

"Let's just rent a room."

"If we're paying rent, I'll never have enough money to finish high school."

So I gave money to Juana for the weekly food budget again, and the rest of what I earned to Maximo. He bought bricks, cal and cement, and leveled the roof. Juana took down the rooftop clotheslines and cleaned out the racks of empty soda bottles.

"*Estará bien padre*," Maximo said as he sketched the windowed dome he would make, and the picture window overlooking the soccer field and trash-strewn arroyo below the house. I told myself it would be very cool indeed, like Maximo said, an apartment all to ourselves. My clothes all in one place, a door to close, a rocking chair in the corner. A rocking chair—my throat constricted sadly.

"Another opportunity will come along. I had two miscarriages between the four of you," my mother said from New Jersey. "I'm sure it's for the best."

I heard her double meaning. Maybe now you'll be done with this little Mexican adventure and come on home and find an appropriate man to marry and have a baby with, not a youngster who hasn't finished high school.

///

My midwife, Alice, said we should wait six months before trying to conceive again. I bartended, wrote tourism brochures, took a mentally retarded girl to a hot springs pool for money, and looked for other jobs, desperate to make a nest before I got pregnant again. I jumped at the chance to go to a party in Los Balcones, let loose, speak English, stop worrying. "What for?" Carlos said when I mentioned the party, but I ignored the fact that he clammed up around other Americans and convinced him to go with me.

Pulling up to the house, I lurched the van Gussie had lent me forward and back in the same frantic way I ran around looking for jobs. A long metal squeak like a saxophone bleat filled the air, then a crunch, and Carlos jumped out, scowling. There was a meter-long scratch, like the musical note that had just been struck, on the side door.

"You don't know how to drive!" Carlos shouted. "This is crazy. I'm not going to that party. I hate gringo parties."

He hurried down the hill on foot. I had *not* gotten dressed to only go back to that sardine can of a house. I went inside.

The gathering was a Sagittarius party—the invitees had late November-December birthdays, like I did. I drank rum and Coke, danced across from a drunken guy in socks and watched Gussie's therapist run his hands through her hair. I left after midnight, and drove Gussie's damaged van through the streets of Colonia San Antonio like an injured animal making its way stealthily through the dark. I parked over the drainpipe and wobbled down the hill in high shoes.

"*Ya llegué*," I said softly as I entered the lamina-roofed house, directing my voice through the broken window into Juana and Maximo's room to inform them I was not an intruder but someone who belonged in the house and that I was home.

But I still didn't feel that I belonged, now even less that I no longer carried Carlos' child. I barely made enough money to live. And my boyfriend, did he want me anymore? He'd left me alone at a party over a bad parking job. I was stuffing down a panic as well. Gussie had said, "Oh well, things happen," when I told her about her van. But I felt obligated to repair the dent and I had no extra money.

I squeezed toothpaste onto my toothbrush and pulled my jacket closer around me. The water coming from the patio sink was icy. I brushed and brushed; putting off the moment I would go down and face the man who had walked away from me. If he yelled or dismissed me, it would be my sign to pack my bags. I was glad my parents could not see me at this moment, descending cement stairs in the dark, feeling along a stone wall to make my way, my fingers afraid of finding spiders, shivering because half the house was open to the night cold, all so I could be with Carlos. With the man/boy who didn't want to go to gringo parties with me, who wouldn't speak to me because I'd dented a car—who didn't want to grow up.

The miscarriage was a sign to return to my country. The scratched van was a sign. I thought of Carlos' back, his hunched shoulders as he walked away from me. *He left me alone*, I said to myself, so I could be angry, and not feel the enormous sadness, *la tristeza,* that beat below my breastbone when I thought of leaving him.

I pushed open the door and crept into the room. The reading light I'd hung on a nail over the bed flicked on. Carlos lay blinking at me from under the blankets, still dressed in his clothes, like he'd slept as a child, like he'd slept all his life until he met me. Hugo's and Dulce's beds were empty.

I sat next to Carlos and tried to say that I was leaving. Back to the house in South Philly, to Sunday dinners at my parents, to finishing and trying to find a publisher for my book. Back to giving cab drivers directions in English, to long nights with rented videos instead of Mexican telenovelas. I fingered the edge of a blanket. Carlos sat up and leaned against the brick wall. For a few minutes, neither of us spoke.

"Carlos," I began. "The van, you know, I'm sorry. I've already talked to Gussie about it. She's not too upset."

He looked at the wall. Tears welled in his eyes. How did he know what I was going to say next?

"Carlos," I whispered and my arms went around him. His shoulders heaved and he punched the bed.

"*Yo quiero a mi niño,*" he said. I want my baby.

I had stopped thinking about the lost baby, according to my family's unwritten code. Unpleasant feelings? Ignore them, get over them. Somewhere inside of me, though, I knew I grieved too. "I wanted our baby," Carlos said, his body going slack. He closed his eyes. His cheeks were wet. I wiped his tears with the back of my hand.

"We'll have another one," I whispered—my family's response—make everything better. Did I mean it? Then something unlocked inside of me. I felt sadness too. I was sad that the great joy I'd felt to be carrying a baby had disappeared. I felt anxious that I was 34-years old and might not get another chance. The pregnancy had made all our troubles together bearable. I was sad that feeling was gone. I stroked Carlos' hair as if comforting myself. Carlos let me hold him. He switched off the light, and we rocked back and forth in the dark.

///

Pino and Pancho Reyes were look-alike brothers with matching matchstick legs emerging from giant basketball shorts and disappearing again into giant Air Jordans. They had oversized hands that spun, dribbled, rolled and flipped basketballs back and forth while they spoke. Hugo and Carlos called them Los Pinos. Pancho, the younger, had thick eyebrows that made him look like all the Irish kids I grew up with, except a shade darker. The Pinos came in from Guanajuato every Thursday to play for the Ring team in the park. After, they spent the night in Juana's house and lately had begun staying until Monday, sharing the room with us.

It was Thursday and, sure enough, a clatter of feet on the steps announced their arrival. I sat on the edge of Carlos' bed, where I had been watching a telenovela blissfully alone before the two sets of brothers entered. I strained to hear the anxious voices of the señoras on the television, and the maid's frantic, whispered phone call.

"Did you win?" I asked my boyfriend halfheartedly and in English. I wasn't happy about the invasion.

Pancho, in his Ring team uniform, lit a cigarette by the blanketed window, pulling the cover aside and blowing smoke out into the night.

"*Estuvo pésimo el arbitraje.*" Hugo, across from me on his bed, uttered some more choice complaints about the referee.

Carlos sat next to me and put his hand on my leg, which I usually found endearing, but now had the urge to shake off.

"*Pinches gordos del Don Pedro ni se pueden mover,*" Carlos laughed, good-naturedly insulting the other team.

"*Pinche Michael Jordan. World's best athlete,*" Pino said, jiggling an unlaced Air Jordan.

I couldn't hear the telenovela, so I switched it off and, irritated, pulled a book from the shelf.

I was in a room with four men who could not legally drink in most states north of the border. Carlos' father worked on our upstairs apartment on weekends. The floor was laid, but there were no windows or doors. The bathroom lacked fixtures. It would take months of weekend work before we had a place of our own.

Los Pinos stretched out on foam rubber mats on the floor. When they took their shoes off, the room filled with an odor so thick it was almost visible. The basketball talk continued even after the lights were out. I had talked basketball when I was a teenager because it got me attention from boys. I didn't want to talk sports anymore, and suddenly a startling truth was clear to me—I was still in the middle of a macho culture that ignored women. I was repeating my own disappointing life.

But maybe I wasn't. Carlos pulled me to lean into him. He held me tight.

"*Y tu, que opines?* What do *I* think? *"Quien fue major*—Magic Johnson or Larry Bird?" Carlos asked me. The room waited for my answer.

I don't have an opinion, I wanted to say. I don't have passion for the N.B.A. any more.

"All around player—Magic, no doubt," I said. My father had coached Johnson for thirteen games in L.A., until he fell off the bicycle, and he adored Magic for his love of basketball, fondness for fans, and his genuine good-guy-ness and for the infectious spirit with which he infused the team. So, if my dad liked Magic, I liked Magic.

"Larry Bird, clutch player," Carlos argued.

"Hey, no English," Pancho said in English. "*Voy con ella*. Magic."

"*Ya ves?*" I said to Carlos. See? "You don't know anything! And where'd you learn words like 'clutch player'?"

"I know a lot of things you don't know about," he teased, pulling me close.

"Bill Walton," Hugo said.

"Bill Walton *healthy*." I argued. It occurred to me I *was* in the mix. In the locker room. Super-macho or not, at least in Mexico, I wasn't shut out.

Macho didn't exactly refer to a swaggering guy who ate while the woman stood by his chair, although heaven knew that existed—one only had to look at Gerónimo and Lupe. The macho in Mexican culture, an Instituto professor had explained back when I could afford Spanish classes, referred to how the men are completely spoiled by their mothers.

My hand had shot up. "That would make a bunch of useless men," I'd concluded. Of course, back then it was only theory.

Now I was determined Carlos would not be the living example of the useless man theory, although by all indications, like the fact that he had never in his entire life made his own bed, he was.

When an older American couple I knew mentioned they needed moving help, I said I had just the person for them. Carlos went over early one Saturday morning and by the end of the day had earned a refrigerator. We put it in the smaller of the two rooms Maximo was building.

Dulce had gone out and it was early in the week, so there were no Pinos. We went to sleep alone. I dreamed of glass windows in the yawning open spaces of the room, of paint on the walls, of large square brick-colored tiles on the uneven cement floor. I began to dream of a rocking chair in the corner again, of cooking potatoes and carrots and mashing them with boiled water into baby soup.

One day I came home from the publicity office where I worked writing copy and found the refrigerator warm and humming in our half-done room. A hook had been pushed into the ceiling, and the refrigerator's cord ascended like a happy tail. From the ceiling it was connected to a series of electrical extensions that ran along the walls until it reached Juana's naked kitchen bulb and was plugged into a socket at the bulb's base. Inside the freezer were some two-dozen *arroz con leche* popsicles in little plastic cups with wooden sticks tilting to the sides.

I went into our unfinished big room, sat on a plastic chair and opened *Tinisima,* about the talented Italian photographer who was Edward Weston's model and who ran with Diego Rivera and the Communist art crowd in Mexico City in the twenties. I read about the dinner parties they threw and imagined little parties in my new space.

Juana ascended the steps as I turned the page. She withdrew two rice-milk *paletas* from the refrigerator. Minutes later two of Carlos' nieces came up and took two more. Then came three neighborhood kids, giggling and holding each other to find courage to walk past the gringa with her feet up on the cement bag.

"Go away," I said under my breath, and went back to my book. The kids shrieked and ran from the doorway back down the stairs, clutching their popsicles.

"How many? Three? One thousand five hundred pesos." I heard Juana making change from a plastic bag filled with heavy coins. I closed my book. I would never bring my friends up to my little roost for guacamole and beer. They would have to walk past the scattering of empty Coke bottles, Cafe Legal wrappers on the floor, the shaver with the rusting blade in the planter, the chicken poop.

With our refrigerator connected, Juana bought milk

days in advance. Her popsicle business thrived. It was my cue that even having our own room wouldn't guarantee privacy, but I ignored it. If I had opened my eyes, I would have had to leave my boyfriend, and I wasn't ready to.

BLACK EYE

"Want me to put the tortillas on?" Carlos asked, washing paint off his hands at the sink. A pot of frijoles bubbled on the stove. The rice hissed, almost done. I put a salad on the mesquite table, ecstatic to be serving myself greens for the first time in weeks.

We were house sitting in a large two-story house that came with an airy tiled kitchen. The neighborhood of Guadiana didn't have kids who needed their noses wiped in the streets. The owner, a dark-haired woman from Phoenix, had gone to Arizona to sell San Miguel crafts. Carlos was making Christmas ornaments in her "workshop"—a space under an outdoor passage arch—for all the orders she was going to get.

I wore a simple Gap dress with clogs. I put the lid on the rice and turned the heat off. Carlos wrapped tortillas in a cloth. He was in his bare feet and his shirt was untucked.

"Don't you want to go with me?" I asked as we sat.

"No." Carlos spread a tortilla with frijoles and rolled it into a tube.

"I feel better with you at my side."

"You go with Gussie. I'm going to stay here and paint." Carlos indicated the worktable with his hand.

I taxied to Gussie's new apartment. Gussie wore a short dress too. Men whistled at us as we walked up Calle Correo and it made me edgy. I didn't feel the least bit single any more. I hadn't walked at night without Carlos in so long, I'd forgotten what it was like.

What I did crave was speaking in English.

"So, the new boy?" I asked.

"So sweet! He's a waiter at Mama Mia's. His teeth need some work. My dad's a dentist. He can fix him up."

The party was on Calle Chiquitos, near the Jardín. Most of the guests were stargazing on the roof when we arrived. With my back against the crumbling roof ledge and beer in hand, I struck up a conversation with a guy who'd come to San Miguel to write.

"Ha! That used to be me," I told him.

Then the night breeze became chilly and I pulled my jean jacket closer around me. I found Gussie, who was listening to the owner of the house tell about its construction.

"Want to go?" I asked as politely as I could.

"You saved me," she whispered as we waved goodbye to the hostess. "You want to know what roof tile costs?"

"No."

We left, closing the iron gate.

"Let's go to Mama Mia's. I want to wait for Toño," Gussie said.

"Nah, I just want to go home," I said. The breeze had died and the night was still and full of stars. It was almost midnight. Cab drivers lounged against their green taxis along the Jardín curb.

"Well, see ya!" Gussie entered the restaurant. I turned down Calle Aldama and passed the darkened doorways with their iron knockers.

The park was dark as I passed, the courts for once not ringing with bouncing basketballs. I passed Calle Nueva and headed up the Prolongación to where the street narrowed, and realized muted footsteps were falling behind me. My pulse raced while my mind tried to stay calm. But the steps were falling harder and more quickly behind me, and I was shocked but not surprised when an arm went around my neck and pulled me back. I was pressed against a small form, not much bigger than I. Fear surged through my body as I twisted. I saw thick black hair and a young face with a soft mustache trying to come in at the corner of the mouth. He looked younger than Carlos. He pushed my head down and groped my breasts and I saw his green cut-off T-shirt rise above the waist of his man's pants with a faux-leather belt through its loops. A line of dark menacing hair ran from the top of his pants to his navel and I understood that he was not just a boy but a man who wanted to do me harm.

"*Ayúdame!*" Help me*! "Ayúdame!*" I screamed. He gripped the top of my arms hard. We faced each other like adversaries in an angry quarrel. His feet were planted apart and I brought my leg back again and again, trying to land a blow to his groin. But his hold was steely and my kicks rose and fell uselessly. His face contorted as I continued to scream. He turned me and pulled me against him again so my buttocks were against his erection, and I was facing the calm street. I prayed for a car with headlights blazing. "Ayúdame!" I screamed, my throat going hoarse.

He covered my mouth with his hand. I sucked two fingers into my mouth and bit down as hard as I could. He tried to pull his fingers out but that only allowed my teeth to imbed further. My feet kicked out wildly. His legs moved this way and that, avoiding my blows, and we did a shuffling dance across the street as we fought, my screams muffled by his hand in my mouth. With a grunt, he wrenched his fingers from my mouth and yanked his hand down to his side. When it came up again, it was curled into a fist that slammed into my eye. My legs buckled and yellow lights danced in front of me. When my vision cleared, I was looking at the night sky. I was on the ground. My dress was pushed up to my waist and my attacker was standing over me with his hand in my underpants, fishing around my privates with his eyes half closed. I could see he was off guard and that I had a chance to attack back but my ears were ringing, my head was pounding with pain and my arms would not raise themselves up even though I willed them to. I'm done, I thought bitterly.

Had a minute passed? Five? The stucco wall next to my face was painted mustard yellow. There was broken glass under my elbow. I willed my arm to move again, and it did. My fingers curled over a sharp piece of glass while my attacker fumbled with his belt with one hand. His face was twisted, his eyes lost in a violent world.

I realized I would retch if his finger went inside me one more time. I dropped the glass and gripped the wrist of the hand that plunged into my panties. "Motherfucker!" I screamed. I rolled to my side. My movement surprised him and in that unguarded moment, I dizzily got to my feet.

"Help me!" I yelled at the street, staggering. He grabbed my wrist and pulled me toward him. I wrenched my arm down to free it but there was little strength in my movements. He pushed me against the adobe wall and held me there with an arm across my chest. His hair, which had been pushed back, fell down over his eyes and his breath came in quick spurts. His free arm went back and his hand closed into a fist. I closed my eyes and turned my head. Then the night air was blowing softly over me, the pressure on my chest lifted and my wrist was throbbing but free.

I heard footsteps running over the cobblestones, diminishing. I heard deep, gasping breaths and realized it was me. I felt like I could not get enough air into my lungs, so I dropped my head to my knees and saw my panties sticking out from the bottom of my dress. Disgust flooded over me as I pulled them up. I saw my shoe in the street and took a step toward it. My muscles felt as if they'd been pulled off my bones.

"Are you all right?" said a floating voice. I looked up but could only see from one eye.

"Compared to what?" I said.

"Come with me," the woman said. She was dressed in gray sweatpants with a matching zip-up sweatshirt and unlaced sneakers. I followed her up the street and saw people in doorways and a couple in bathrobes out on a second floor balcony watching me make my way over the cobblestones. Why had it taken them so long to open doors?

"Sit here," the woman said when we'd entered a house halfway up the block, indicating a mesquite bench. "There's the bathroom if you'd like."

I leaned on the sink with arms that shook. My mouth was open in an O as I still tried to gulp air deeply into my lungs. In the bathroom mirror, I saw that the small glittery clip I'd pushed into my hair at eyebrow level was gone, I was wearing only one earring and my left eye was swelling shut. I put my hand to my head and felt around. My hair was matted in the back like a hospital patient's. "I guess I'm not all right," I whispered.

"Here," the woman said handing me a glass of water when I came out. "Were you screaming?"

I nodded and brought the glass of water to my mouth with two hands.

"It was so high-pitched I thought it was dogs having sex," she said. "I've called the police. They should be here any minute now."

Walking alone by the park at midnight in a short dress. Now I felt stupid. I didn't want to suffer snide looks from Mexican cops.

Two minutes later they were at the door, two young men in blue uniforms. "What did he look like?" He wasn't mocking me.

"Young," I said. "Green T-shirt, black pants."

"Will you come with us to look for him?"

We circled the park and from the back of the white VW patrol car I saw that the basketball courts were a black hole. The clean-shaven officer aimed a spotlight and the black geometric figures turned into square-cut bushes and trees.

"Oh," I said suddenly. "He'll have bite marks on his fingers."

I was glad when the searchlight didn't turn anything up. What if they had? They'd put him in the back seat with me?

"We'll take you home," the mustached one said. At the end of Calle Jacaranda, I pointed to the Phoenix lady's door. Relief poured through me as I stepped into the light that flooded the doorway. Somehow my keys were still in my pocket and I opened the door.

"Gracias," I said to the police. They were standing by the door to see me into the house.

A light burned in the front room but the house was empty. It was 1:10 A.M. I pulled jeans out of the cedar closet and put them on with an old sweatshirt. I rolled my dress up, put it in a plastic bag and stuffed it into the bottom of the kitchen trashcan. I sat on a living room chair and hugged my knees

Then keys clicked in the front door and Carlos walked in. His hair was down over his eyes and he was breathing hard. "I've been out on the street looking for you!" he panted. "You didn't come home. I didn't even know where your pinche party was."

"I was attacked," I whispered.

"What?" Carlos stood still, keys dangling from his hand.

"I was walking home with Gussie, and she wanted to stop in Mama Mia's, so I kept walking. A guy grabbed me as I passed Calle Nueva."

"You walked past the park alone at this hour?" Carlos' voice was tight.

I nodded my head miserably. "He tried to rape me." I lifted my head to look him in the eyes.

"And?" Carlos flicked the keys back and forth.

"And I fought and fought until a lady finally came out of her house," I said. Carlos' eyes pinballed around the room.

"So, he did or he didn't?"

"He didn't." The question exhausted me. "Why is that the important point?"

Carlos stepped toward me, and peered at my eye. His arm went back and I flinched but did not move. His keys flew across the room and hit the glass face of a clock, and a fissure opened from five after to twenty-five of.

Carlos kicked an antique chest and when the chest didn't move, he went into the dining room and turned over all the wooden chairs at the large mesquite table. In the kitchen he opened cabinets and threw several drinking glasses against the tiled wall. The last glass hit an iron door pull and burst, tinkling to the floor like a thousand frayed nerves. I slumped into the easy chair. I felt dulled, unable to move, only capable of viewing the continuing violence.

I went upstairs and sat on the edge of the big bed, staring at a Oaxacan rug. When Carlos came up, he did not look at me. He stepped around me, and sat on the other side of the bed, facing the opposite wall. Then he lay back and stared at the ceiling. When I turned around to look, his eyes were closed, not peacefully as in sleep, but squeezed shut with the effort of blocking me out.

I went into a different bedroom, lay on an unsheeted mattress and stared at the ceiling beams. My boyfriend who adored me couldn't look at me. We were in separate rooms on separate beds. Carlos was letting me down in the most finalizing way imaginable.

I had walked past the park mindlessly, thinking only of getting home to him. I was guilty of being stupid. And nothing else. Why did that make my boyfriend so angry he couldn't speak?

I couldn't stay with him. Tears rolled from my eyes and onto the mattress until little wet pools formed by my ears. I would leave just as I came. I would look for a job in Philly to fill my days. I wouldn't care what it was.

Then my feet hit the floor. Who did he think he was to shut me out like the smell of trash? I flew into the next room where Carlos lay on the giant bed, unmoving, eyes still clenched shut. "It was so bad!" I yelled in a voice I didn't recognize. "It was so bad!" I screamed it a dozen more times. I was on the bed, kneeling next to him, raining blows on his chest with my fists. "It was terrible! You have no idea!" Carlos let me hit him.

"And," I said in an exhausted voice, "it wasn't the first time."

Carlos looked at me, his body still. I sat back on my heels, breathing hard. The moon came in from the window under which a rooster crowed every dawn.

"Tell me," Carlos said. I couldn't tell if his voice was accusing or compassionate. The accusations were what I had feared for fourteen years. Of being utterly stupid. Of not knowing that girl in Los Angeles who went to the party with me was one of the best-known player groupies in the NBA. Of bringing the attack upon myself by not understanding what the men had on their minds. The familiar rush of anxiety raced through my body.

"No," I said.

"Tell me." His voice was softer.

I hadn't told anyone. I'd been sure something bad would happen to my father and my world would end if I did.

"An NBA player tried to rape me when I was nineteen," I said dully. "I fought him off too."

In an emotionless voice, I told him about the party on Rodeo Drive I'd gone to in my father's place, when he'd been home recovering from a head injury and coma. I told him about the girl I went with, to whom I'd been introducted by my dad's assistant coach, and the player and his friend in a white suit, all of them holding the Marriott Hotel elevator doors open for me. What did it matter?

I told Carlos about the agent who called me on the phone the next day as I tried to sit normally at a family dinner, and how he'd threatened to ruin my father's career in the NBA if I told.

"Since then, I'll be doing something normal – talking to friends, writing a story, serving a beer—and this trembling comes over me, and I'm sure everybody can see it, then I realize, nobody can. All I've wanted since that day is for someone to understand what it was like for me." I laughed bitterly.

"You couldn't have ruined your father's career. You know that, don't you?"

I stared at the brick-colored wall. Of course it was true. How, in all those years, had I not realized it?

"I didn't understand that then."

"No. That's what that asshole agent was counting on."

I snuck a look at Carlos. He was gazing glumly at his knees. He didn't seem to be working up any accusations.

"I'm not mad at you. I'm mad at me," Carlos punched

his thigh. "I'm mad I wasn't there to walk you home. I wish I'd been there when you were nineteen."

I was shivering. Carlos touched my leg tentatively, then, encircled my shoulders. He moved his body close to mine, until I was leaning against his warmth. "My brave, brave girl," he whispered. I nestled my face in the smooth skin under his neck and felt I could stay there a very long time. Carlos rubbed my back under my sweatshirt. I began to feel warm.

The rooster from next door crowed.

"Let's make love like human beings," Carlos whispered. He touched me like I was made of crystal. Later, under an early morning sun, we slept.

DEFENDED

Ministerio Público was connected to the jail. I focused with the one eye that wasn't swollen shut when I signed in at the guardhouse the next morning. The night before the police had picked up José Ramirez, a 17-year old from a San Miguel neighborhood famous for tin and iron workshops, but also for unemployment and glue-sniffing. José Ramirez was in the Corral Bar on Calle Insurgentes, gulping down his fourth rum and coke when the police demanded to see his fingers, in which they found deep bite marks. Now I had to press charges.

A freshly shaved *policia* roused us from sleep and told me to be at the Ministerio Publico at 9 A.M., which we were. The secretaries who were to take my statement didn't come in until 10 however, and Carlos and I sat on folding chairs against the wall, watching two *federales* in their twenties run around the office importantly with pistols sticking out from the back of their jeans. Carlos kept his arm around me.

Soon a guard came in leading a handcuffed José Ramirez, still in his green T-shirt and black pants. "That's him," I told Carlos, who stiffened and sat up. The teen was shown to a chair in the room across from us, where he sat with his head hanging on his chest.

He looked so short, so young. I could see the fake stitches in his cheap shoes. A hot flash of anger at God passed through me that I, a woman, could not even overpower a short skinny teenager, who in the light of day looked feeble and scared.

The federal agent at a metal desk in the room snapped shut a folder, stood and exited the room.

"I'm going to get a drink of water," Carlos said in an even voice. He entered the room with the metal desk, passed in front of the handcuffed teen, took a paper cone and filled it with water. With his back to the boy, and to me across the room, he drank the water and crushed the cup.

Carlos threw the cup in the trash, turned and took the boy's hair in one hand. He shook José Ramirez's head, banging it against the wall. From across the room, I saw Carlos' arm going back and forth, and heard a series of dull thuds. After a few minutes, one of the twenty-something federal agents went into the room and said calmly, "Ya, ya, ya." Carlos released the boy's head and returned to his seat at my side.

"They left you in there with him for a long time," I whispered.

"Didn't you see how they all went out of the room? They were giving me my chance," Carlos replied. I felt oddly inflated. Valued. Nobody had ever landed blows for me before.

Finally the secretaries came in, and I told them all I could remember about being grabbed, punched and pushed to the ground. They cracked gum and took down my words on clacking manual typewriters without looking at me. The lady in the gray sweatsuit came and stated that she'd heard me scream and found me shoeless and gasping.

Carlos and I bought sliced *bifstek* on the way home. We spotted Gussie, Hugo and El Sexy on different street corners, and invited them over. In the house, Carlos threw the beef into a pan with sliced onions, and soon Hugo was assembling a big plate of tacos. José Ramírez was in jail, and I felt good. I had given my statement and been believed. We drank beer, and my friends got used to my black eye and stopped staring at it. I laughed. I fetched salsa. I served more beer.

The next day I was in the center of town at dusk. I was wearing dark sunglasses at Carlos's request, so people wouldn't think he'd hit me. I didn't like being stared at either, so I kept the glasses on, but I couldn't see. Walking down Calle Hernandez Macias, I tripped on a flagstone and caught myself on a brick wall. I took my glasses off, began to cry and put them back on. Dark was falling fast; it put me in a panic. Colonia San Antonio and the house with the lamina roof were half a world away. Oh, please, please, (I wouldn't say God, I was still mad at him) just let me get there. What kind of a fool had a boyfriend without a phone? Footsteps fell behind me and I stifled a scream and stepped into the street so at least I would be seen when I was grabbed. Car lights blinded me; a car horn blasted. I jumped onto the curb. It was seven o'clock at night.

I made my way down Calle Codo in my dark glasses, hugging walls, cursing the universe. People entered Espino Market and exited with bags of groceries. The guy swinging down the steps with a six-pack did graphic design work for Lucy.

"José Luís!" I called. "José Luís."

"Hey, Susan." He lifted the six-pack, offering a can. The gesture was so normal, I started crying, hugging my arms to my chest.

"Caray, I thought you liked beer," José Luís asked, stepping toward me. I took my glasses off, and he rocked back on his heels. "Susan, what happened to you?"

"I was attacked by the park two nights ago. I don't feel like myself. Could you walk me home?"

José Luís opened his car door, brushed papers off the seat and drove me to the drainpipe.

"Thanks," I said, wiping my face.

Just then, Carlos came out from the store where we bought cakes and milk. "*Que onda?*"

José Luís jumped out of the car, hurried around and opened my door. Carlos nodded at José Luís but was staring at me.

"*Cuídala,*" Jose Luis said. Take care of her. He stepped back, and Carlos put his arm around my shoulders. If Lupe ever came home in a car with another guy—as if Lupe knew anyone who owned a car—Gerónimo would beat the guy up. I was sure of that. And, probably her too.

"*Orale,*" Carlos said. He probably would have given José Luís a barrio handshake, but he had his arm around me. In bars, Mexican men treated you like some prize they would get if they fought hard enough among themselves. But now, from cops to Carlos' brothers and friends, I was being shown a respect that surprised me.

Carlos walked me away from the drainpipe and toward the Instituto. "I can't see," I said.

"Take your glasses off. Nobody can see your eye in the dark." Soon we were approaching the park.

"Carlos," I said, slowing my steps.

"We're going back there and we're walking down that street. If we don't, you won't want to walk on the street ever again."

"Don't let go of me."

"I got you."

We walked past the park and up the street, like I had that night. Light glowed in the windows of the houses. Geraniums on the second floor balconies made dull pink spots against the night, and the adobe wall I'd been pushed against was crumbling in a rather charming manner as if the tourism department had planned it that way.

Back in the house, Hugo called Carlos into a down-stairs huddle. When he came up, he said that this is what they'd planned—they would find José Ramirez when he was released on bail, cut his testicles off and dump them among some faraway cactuses.

"More violence," I said. "Just what we need." We were in the kitchen. Hugo had just taken off to find some guy he knew who had a truck, for rapist transportation, once he was ball-less. I secretly liked the plan, but the peacenik side of me wouldn't go for it. "You'll end up in jail. Then what'll I do? I'd have to go home, I guess."

"Shh! Don't say that." He sighed. "Chingao. I sure would like to beat that guy senseless."

"You already did, remember?" Carlos had come out of the downstairs room pounding the wall with his fist, Hugo behind him clapping his hands as if firing up before a ball game. Now he looked defeated.

"I don't want you to get in trouble. Just leave it."

"I'll guess, sooner or later, he'll get his," he said.

///

"Let's go to the park," Carlos said. He bounced the basketball on the kitchen floor. If I were my mother, I'd have told him to take it outside. We were back in the Guad-diana house, scheduled to stay a week more.

I sighed. "My muscles still hurt. I wish I had a good book. I just want to stay in the house."

If I went outside without dark glasses, I was stared at. I still could not stand to hear footsteps behind me, no matter what time of day. "You go." I picked at a cuticle.

"I'll bring home some chicken and make you dinner later." The ball rang off the flagstones as Carlos dribbled it down the path to the gate.

I needed to make money if I was to stay in Mexico. A guy I knew earned four hundred dollars a shot writing erotic short stories for a porn magazine. I'd thought before I would try it, but now the idea made me sick. I was so tired of struggling – a modeling job here, a party bartending job there, money in my hand then gone. Philadelphia kept popping into my head.

"Let's go out to lunch," Gussie said on the phone.

"I don't have any money and I don't want to go out until my eye heals," I said.

"Then stay there. I'm coming over."

Minutes later, Gussie was heating spaghetti she'd made the night before on the stove.

I leaned in the doorway while she stirred the sauce with a wooden spoon. "I want to go back to Philly," I told her. The spoon stopped mid-round.

"I keep thinking of Chicago too," she whispered. "Of Sunday afternoons, the sound of a football game on TV. A roast in the oven at my mother's house."

"Mashed potatoes." I said dreamily.

"Sailing on Lake Michigan!"

"Fall! Crisp air. Raking up a pile of leaves," I said, laying forks on straw placemats. "Every Sunday the Philadelphia Inquirer has a classified section this big," I held my thumb and forefinger as wide apart as they would get.

"I like my kids, but I'm getting real tired of earning a hundred dollars a week."

"I'm so pathetic I'm house sitting because I can't afford to pay rent."

"I haven't seen snow in four years." Gussie sighed, carrying two steaming bowls to the table.

"Carlos?" Gussie asked.

"He loves me but doesn't have a job. Your new boy-friend?"

"Toño is the nicest guy I've ever dated, here or any-where. Do you know he's waitering to save money to go back to school and get his masters in Cactology."

I raised my eyebrows.

"Well, whatever it's called. Scientists don't even know how many classes of cactus exist in Mexico. He wants to be one of the first people ever to catalogue the different types."

We ate glumly. Finally, in our thirties, we had nice boyfriends, but no money.

"Sit and keep me company," I said, when we had fin-ished. "You cooked. I wash." But as I plunged my hands into the soapy water, the sink full of dishes blurred in front of me. As I tried to steady myself, I threw up into the sink.

YOU ARE MY SUNSHINE

I was thinking about how, growing up, I saw my dad as Superman, Spiderman and Speed Racer all in one. Why wouldn't I? His name was in the paper all the time. People called him a winner. But lately I was thinking how my dad was just a guy. A guy in a T-shirt who tried to sneak out to play basketball on Saturday mornings when he was a young father, until my mom told him he had to take me out in the stroller instead. A guy who whistled when he slapped on Old Spice. A guy who'd flop on a sled and let all the neighborhood kids pile on top of him. A guy who taught me to ride a bicycle.

Later, I thought I wanted my father to *see* me. Maybe that's why I'd gotten a job as a television news reporter. I was feeling lately, though, that maybe I hadn't had to have worked so hard at getting noticed.

My father had just called to say that since I was pregnant, he wanted to give us a wedding. "Your mother," he said then stopped.

"My mother, what?"

"I'll tell you another time."

"Tell me."

"Aw, you know your mother. She got everyone on the phone and wanted to cook up a plan to get you out of there."

"Everyone?"

"Conference call. Now that she's in real estate, she knows how to do that kind of thing, you know."

I swallowed. "And?"

"I told her if you're still down there, you must be happy." There was a pause. "Are you happy?"

"You stuck up for me, Dad. Didn't you?"

"I said if you were going to have a baby, then your mind was made up and our job was to throw a wedding."

"Dad." I wanted to say, *you're my hero*, but the words got stuck in my throat.

⫻

A pink satin matador's jacket hung near the entrance of the restaurant we'd booked for the rehearsal dinner. Booked was a broad term. When I went in and asked for a reservation for twelve, the owner pushed his daughter's Barbie dolls off the table, handed me a menu and shrugged. Nonetheless, tables had been pushed together to make a long banquet row for us. My relatives shook water off their shoulders and pulled out chairs. I'd stood in the rain by their bed and breakfast and hailed four cabs for everyone. Four seats remained for Carlos, his mother and father and perhaps Hugo.

"I think this calls for drinks," Aunt Ann, my mother's sister said. "Whew, the shopping in this town!"

"I don't think there's anything left in the stores," said Dorothy, my father's aunt.

The waitress came to take our order. "*Al rato*," I said. In a moment.

"The margaritas!" said Aunt Mary Jean. "I had to take an afternoon nap!" My sister arched an eyebrow.

The waitress appeared again. "Appetizers?" said Aunt Ann hopefully.

"Sure, appetizers. Carlos and his parents will be here any minute," I said.

Plates of queso fundido came and were passed around. I showed everyone how to eat the cheese with tortillas. Then the plates were cleared. My father drummed his fingers on the table. I watched the door.

"Maybe the rain has held them up," my mother said brightly. "Yes," I said, and checked the entrance again as if Carlos and his mother and father would walk in any minute, but suddenly I knew they wouldn't and I knew that I'd known it all along.

"I think we should order," I said.

"A toast to Susan." That was the best my mother could do, and I was happy with it. Then Aunt Dorothy giggled, "To the groom!"

Stars were peeking through the clouds when we left the restaurant, and the night had turned breezy. We walked in twos down the narrow street, looking for taxis. "Well," my mother said to the sky, "never heard of a rehearsal dinner without the future husband."

Carlos was waiting for us at the bottom of the staircase as we entered the house where we were staying in Guadiana. The Arizona lady had invited us not only to have the wedding there, but to occupy some rooms for a few days.

"Where were you?" I cried.

"It was raining buckets, and cabs don't come into our neighborhood in the rain. You know my mother and her legs. I couldn't expect her to walk down that hill and over to Canal." His fingers gripped the banister.

"His mother has arthritis in her legs. She would have had to walk half a mile in the rain to get a taxi. That's why they didn't come," I explained to my parents in English. "Men in this culture look out for their mothers and their women." Here was my chance. I could tell them about the kid who grabbed me by the park, how Carlos had banged the kid's head on the wall to show him not to mess with his woman. It would show them the Carlos they weren't seeing, the grownup one. I took a breath. Then I felt sick in my stomach. Maybe it was only the baby, but I bent over and breathed and didn't say anything.

"Get some rest," my father said. He and my mother trod upstairs to their large bedroom. Carlos and I went up the stairs too.

"You could have come yourself." I stared at the whirring ceiling fan.

"I thought I should stay with my mother."

"Do you realize that my relatives came from far away to meet you?" I said. I took a deep breath and patted my stomach. "You are about to make a family with us. This means you put me first."

If he didn't understand, I had to make it clear. It was the only way.

///

The next day, I adjusted my white wedding dress, pulled on pale hose and slipped into Gussie's glimmery white shoes.

"No way," I muttered to myself, wiping my brow. I took the hose off.

"Here, you need more eyeliner," my sister said, turning over her makeup bag. "You should have had a massage."

"Ha! I'm lucky if I get a hot shower most days."

Jen looked at me as if I had dog poop stuck to my shoe.

Below, the first guests were arriving at the garden gate. Some of them actually thought Carlos and I was a charming couple.

"Susan," my father called from downstairs. "Little crisis here."

"What, Dad?"

"Carlos is wearing sneakers."

"Oh."

"I'm going to see if your brother has an extra pair of shoes." I waved an OK and parked myself at the upstairs window. At the gate, my father held Paul in a shoulder lock, explaining in detail where the shoes were, while my brother nodded as if he were in a time-out huddle. Across from the gate, Carlos came out of the casita in dress pants and Adidas basketball shoes and my father sprinted across the yard, past the pomegranate trees and steered him back inside. Then my father stood, handsome in a summer suit, surveying the guys setting up tables and chairs, patting his chest.

"He's looking for his whistle," my sister said, joining me the window. I laughed. I had bitten my fingernails to the quick, watching Carlos turn into his shyest self around my family. I had imagined him and my dad swapping basketball stories. He would invite my father to the park to see a game. They'd walk home chummily, shaking their heads at the reffing, and later, at how my mother and I both fell asleep on the couch watching television. That was before we'd all eaten breakfast on the bougainvillea petal-strewn patio of an old San Miguel hotel, and Carlos hadn't said a word the whole time except for when he whispered to me in Spanish that my brother Paul was pretty funny but he still thought all this fuss over getting married was over the top.

I ignored it. He was nervous. And the Carlos who told jokes and made his brothers laugh? Aliens had taken him and left a personality-less copy in his place.

For the next hour, the garden filled with my friends and family. My father paced. "Susan," he called up the steps.

I went to the landing. "'On time' has a different meaning in Mexico. The judge will come."

"The guests are restless."

"Why don't you open the bar?"

Back in my perch, I spied the waiters lounging near the soda crates, snapping their bow ties at each other. My father strode up and made a motion like shaking a martini, and they hopped up. Soon guests were lining up at the bar.

My sister brought a bottle of white wine upstairs and poured. I put my hand out.

"You're pregnant."

"Half a glass." I went back to the window. My sister, Jen, joined me.

"Who's the lady in the bare feet?"

"She owns this house." I knew that didn't explain much. I knew my sister thought I was still a hippie. "They say her husband used to transport drugs. He was killed in a car crash, along with her son."

Carlos' sister, Dulce, tottered through the gate on high heels carrying a huge pot. She stood looking around. Then my dad appeared and took the pot and carried it to the kitchen. Following Dulce was a hottie they called Ricky Martin.

"Why doesn't her date help her?" Jen asked.

"He's gay," I said.

"Gay men can lift." Jen put her wine glass down and touched my stomach, first with fingertips, then with her whole hand, finding the beginning roundness.

"Anything happening in there?"

"He doesn't start kicking until the fifth month."

"She." Jen looked beautiful, her figure perfect, her blonde hair styled to blow perfectly in the Mexican breeze. She wouldn't want my life. But she wanted a baby. And a husband—not in that order.

Cha-Cha, who did translations in Lucy's office, squeezed into the room, rum and Coke first. "Muchachas, the judge arrived at my wedding at midnight. All the guests were sloshed. The judge was tanked. My husband says he's not sure we got married."

"Don't let my father hear you say that."

Below, my boss at the company that imported medical equipment arrived. He looked like former president Salinas de Gortari, and had whispered to my sister when we visited the office how stunned he was that I, a person with education, could have become engaged to someone so morenito, so low class.

Juana entered next, followed by Maximo, who tugged a borrowed sports coat around him.

"Does anything start on time around here?" my sister asked. About two dozen people would have missed the dum-dum-da-dum if the wedding had started on schedule.

I ran down and found my mother. "Come," I said. My mother followed me over to where Juana and Maximo stood tugging at their clothes. "Mom," I said. "This is Carlos' mother, Juana."

My mother offered her hand. Upper class Mexicans kissed on the cheek. The Ortegas didn't. They didn't touch each other in any way, come to think of it.

"*Susana es buena para mi hijo,*" Juana said, taking my mother's hand finally.

"She says I'm good for her son," I told my mother.

My mother gripped her forearm with her other hand, and they smiled at each other. Mom could feel Juana's kindness, and it was calming her. Call it hormones, or familial love, I was getting teary. I couldn't afford to streak my mascara.

"Juana doesn't hug. She feeds," I told my mom.

"Right," my mother hiccupped. Oh no, she was going to cry too.

"Mom. Want a drink?" I turned to Maximo. "*Quiere una Coca?*"

"Voy." He headed to the bar.

"Ma! *Necesito una olla*," Dulce called from the kitchen door. Her sleeves were rolled up and she was sweating.

"She needs a pan," I explained to my mom. Juana rushed toward the house.

"Are you nervous?" my mother asked.

"No." My mother was the one who was nervous. I just wanted to get on with it and then let everybody get comfortable again. My parents could go out to dinner with my aunts and speak English. Juana could go back to her kitchen and wipe her hands down the front of her T-shirt with no worry and Maximo could get out of his coat and pinchy shoes. I could be alone with Carlos and remember why I loved him.

Earlier in the day, Juana had opened nuts with a hammer in her kitchen, preparing chicken mole for fifty, and told me how she had gotten hitched. There had been a government campaign on the radio to get people living together to marry, she said. She was working as a maid in a rich Mexican lady's house and her boss had said, "Andale, Doña Juana. Why don't you take the day off and get married?"

"So, I thought, why not?" Juana told me. "I went home to Maximo and said, '*Vamonos, viejo*' and we went down to the *registro* and a judge married us."

She had changed her shoes, taken the bus to the centro with her man and signed some papers. Then they'd come home, where she'd left a pot of frijoles on a low boil, and she had sent Dulce up the hill for fresh tortillas.

"How long ago was that?" I'd asked.

"Let's see. Hugo was in *secundaria*." Middle school. "Eh, some four or five years ago." Juana flicked on the blender, grinding the nuts with red chilis.

Gussie was sprawled on the bed, up in the room, balancing her tequila glass on her stomach. "Where's Hugo?

My date the last time we went to a wedding." She laughed. "Remember that chicken? Tasted like tires."

"Remember dancing to ABBA?" I said. I remembered longing to be a bride, to have my life follow a path.

Suddenly the music stopped. Then the violinist started up Solamente Tu. Gussie and Paul's wife scrambled from the bed, straightened their dresses, and ran downstairs. "Good luck," they called over their shoulders.

Jen pinned the flower crown Gussie had brought onto my head. I knew she couldn't understand what I was doing—marrying a guy who couldn't grow a moustache and didn't speak English out loud. I hugged her.

My father cleared his throat loudly in the downstairs hall. I went down and took his arm.

Smiling faces went by in a blur—my mother with tears in the corners of her eyes, my friends craning to see me.

Under the arch, Carlos stood in my brother's shoes, hands clasped in front of him. He looked at me and smiled. I could see he was blocking out everything but me, so I did the same. The father of my child. The words formed in my head, and I remembered. He's going to be a good dad. It's going to be all right.

By ten, the mariachis had come and gone, the Americans, including those who'd been making wagers about how long Carlos and I would last—six months to a year was the going bet—had departed. My mother, from the staircase, had turned, placed both hands on Carlos' shoulders and kissed him on the cheek before she went up. Now, the Ortegas began to arrive.

Hugo's girlfriend wore braces and all but hid behind him. Gerónimo arrived with the girlfriend who wasn't Lupe and a sleepy one year old. Raul and El Sexy pushed open the gate, and then Maximo's brother, who I'd met once when he'd come to the house with a bottle of rum and stayed until it was gone. Tio Beto cracked open a folding chair and said, "*Una cubita para los jovenes!*" A rum and Coke for all the young people!

The wedding party table was filled with men now, and two silent girlfriends. Juana brought plates of mole from the kitchen and set them, one by one, in front of the men. She stood back, and wiped her hands on her dress. "Susana, now you are a señora," Juana said gravely, as if it were the ultimate achievement, and for a fleeting moment, I felt it was. But then I saw that Juana and I stood on the side, while the men sat and talked with their mouths full.

I took a folding chair and squeaked it open next to Carlos. He held my hand. The men were talking about guys who'd had an especially easy time evacuating their bowels after certain Mexican foods, starting with deep fried pork. "*Las carnitas*, Carlos!"

"Pa, *el mole!*"

Maximo's eyes crinkled. Carlos laughed, his personality restored. He signaled to the waiters for beers for his friends. My mind flew up into the clouds. "I'm going to go up."

"*Te acompaño*," Carlos said. I'll go with you. We walked into the big house. Inside, he took my brother's shoes off, and tied on his own tennis shoes.

"You're not going back down there," I said.

"My friends, you know, they *came* after all."

"Your friends don't miss a basketball practice. Now they've come to an open bar event. Big deal."

"El Sexy dressed *up*."

"I don't care about El Sexy. You're married to me. Don't you know anything about a wedding night?"

"I don't know the first thing about weddings."

I sighed. "OK. Learn this." I sang, "*You are my sunshine, my only sunshine.*" I put Carlos' hand on my belly. He hummed along with me. Then he unlaced the sneakers he'd just tied on, and unbuttoned his fancy shirt.

PART II

Movies made in the heyday of the Mexican film industry, during the 1940s and 50s, always ended in a wedding. The swooning bride in white took the arm of the groom, who wore a giant-brimmed charro hat and who had completed some heroic act to win her hand. Often the groom sang. In the background was a white church bedecked with strings of festive paper and cheering villagers. *Fin* appeared in script across the last sequence and it was understood that the couple would live happily ever after—she, making tortillas by hand and he, sauntering around in his fancy cowboy outfit.

Of course, Mexican husband or no, I was not going to live out my days making tortillas. Happily ever after was not my immediate fate. First, I'm not that good at cooking over a fire, and second, Carlos didn't own a charro suit.

Dulce wore striped overalls, like a trainman's, and I, an elastic band skirt, looking not pregnant yet, just like I'd been eating too many tortas. We walked across town, beyond the covered market, to Calzada de la Presa. I'd invited Dulce to go out with me before – to the store, to the centro to mail a letter – and she'd always refused, saying she had to be in the house to serve her father his meals. But we were going to court, and José Ramírez would be there, and we'd all decided it would be better for Carlos not to go and get into any more head slamming.

"Señor Ruiz is your appointed representative or lawyer," a court secretary told me when we entered a room filled with young women at clacking typewriters. My lawyer had a short haircut, an open-necked shirt. He glanced at me briefly, then, winked over my head at one of the office girls.

"We brought these," Dulce said, producing photos Gussie had taken of my bruises after the attack—grip marks at the tops of my arms, the tops of my legs. My left eye bruise was three inches around.

Señor Ruiz looked at the photos, but did not take them from Dulce's outstretched hand. The indifference I'd expected from police—here it was in court.

I was shown to a folding chair at a metal desk just as handcuffed José Ramírez was brought in, followed by a woman in a navy suit. When they sat him across the desk from me, I thought I might pass out from not being able to breathe.

His hair hung low, hiding his eyes. His head fell forward and his shoulders drooped. I couldn't tell if it was with sullenness, defiance, resignation or shame.

A middle-aged woman took the middle chair and began to talk so rapidly that I shook my head in confusion. Dulce translated that the purpose of this hearing was to read our statements back to us and give us the chance to respond to what the other had said at the Ministerio Público three months prior.

Dulce had been in León, visiting her cousin Eva when I'd been attacked. Her fists clenched and unclenched now, as the judge read what I'd said ten hours after being jumped. *Punched, held, hands between my legs, tried to kick him in the groin, fist in my eye.* I began to cry.

"Ya, ya, Sue," Dulce said, patting my arm roughly.

"You've got to see these," Dulce said, holding the photos before the judge's nose. The woman took them and looked through them slowly. Dulce threw my attorney a contemptuous look.

In his statement, José Ramírez claimed he only wanted to walk me home.

"Since when does one have to remove a woman's clothing before walking her home?" Dulce asked loudly.

The judge continued reading. José Ramírez said he hadn't laid a hand on me.

"Those bruises came from La Llorona?" Dulce sputtered.

"She's out of here!" my attorney cried, pointing at Dulce. I stopped crying.

Dulce raised her solidly built frame commandingly, took two steps and stopped. Her arm flew from the side of her body and her fist hit José Ramírez in the jaw. Then she headed for the street door, chest out.

The manual typewriters in the room stopped, and there was a full minute of silence as two dozen eyes watched my sister-in-law cross the room. Then somebody yelled, "She just hit that guy. Get her!" My attorney dashed across the room and grabbed Dulce by the arm.

///

Juana stuffed mashed frijoles into warmed folded tortillas, crumbled ranchero cheese over the beans, and wrapped the tacos in tin foil. She ladled green salsa into a bag. I poured milk into a plastic cup and drank it down in the kitchen, watching her.

"Can I help?" I asked. I still wasn't sure whom she was making dinner for, as everyone I could account for had eaten, and Dulce was in jail.

"No, you rest," Juana said, pouring hot guayaba tea into a washed-out liter yogurt container. I made a mental note to buy Juana a thermos. She dug in her apron pockets like she did for change when she sold homemade popsicles, came up with a ten-thousand peso note.

"Ya," Juana said. She hung her apron on a wire sticking down from the ceiling.

"Ya me voy," Juana called to the house as she exited with a plaid mesh bag laden with the food.

"*Que onda con tu mamá?*" I asked Carlos, back in our downstairs room. What's up with your mom?"

"She can't let Dulce spend the night in jail alone."

Dulce had defended me, and Juana would stand by her. I felt like I belonged to some great clan of warriors, who showed their love for one another by putting up their dukes.

Maybe Dulce liked me, maybe she didn't. I suspected she did and couldn't show it. But no matter what her feelings, now I knew—to Dulce, I was family.

///

The hot metal front door made a hollow sound when somebody banged on it, which people did several times a day. "*Que se le ofrece?*" I asked, using the formal term my boss's wife in the import company employed when asking clients what she could do to help them.

Two dusty kids stared. The girl wore green sweatpants with several long threads unraveling from the waistband, and a sleeveless undershirt. The boy looked to be about eight; he should have been in school. His shoes were oversized and untied. The children wanted fried chicken feet. Juana sold them outside her front door, three for a peso.

Dulce, accompanied by Juana, had spent one night in jail, paid a fine and come home. Dulce normally delivered the bags of chicken feet, hot and greasy from the kitchen. But she had gone for tortillas, so I went into the kitchen to help Juana. Pedro Vargas was singing Ave Maria on the radio; that was how I knew it was noon.

At the door, I took a peso from each child and returned to the kitchen table where I had been cutting toenails off the chicken feet, wondering where the fifty-dollar German knife that I'd given Juana was. An angry red groove was being worn into my hand by Juana's dull serrated knife. I'd watched Juana saw into the tomatoes, carrots and nopales, shaking her hand out, and had retrieved the single good kitchen knife I owned from a box of things to be unpacked when I had my own home. I hadn't seen it since the day I presented it to her.

I wore elastic band shorts, a sleeveless shirt and rubber flip-flops, like Dulce. I hacked at the long, stubborn yellow nails and swatted away flies. Finally three toenails came off at once and I brushed them into the center of the table triumphantly. I watched my hand scoop the nails into a tidy pile and in that instant stepped outside myself and saw a blonde, 35-year old American in a minuscule brick kitchen swarming with flies, cutting the toenails off severed chicken feet. Had I found a purer, simpler life, or sunk into a bacterial existence where extra pesos meant a meal with meat?

We had no phone, no hot water, no space, and little money. The kids on the hill sucked fried chicken feet and didn't wipe their noses. I was five months pregnant and fretted daily about what kind of life we would be offering our child.

Gerónimo and Lupe's two boys were the last babies to have lived in the house, but there were no extra toys, no leftover bottles, no tiny bowls or spoons anywhere. I'd read a magazine article showing necessary items one could expect to collect at a baby shower—blankets, pacifiers, tiny washcloth squares, stuffed bears, walkie-talkie systems, a bowl, spoon and cup set, a baby wipes warmer, and a bath thermometer, all arranged in a pastel basket next to a stroller that would carry two week's worth of groceries as well as an infant.

"My kids never slept in a crib," Juana chuckled, when I reported what the women in the baby class talked about. I *wanted* a pretty crib and delicate pastel clothes.

"How are we going to send this child to college?" I screeched at Carlos one day. "And pay for doctor's appointments, the birth, bottles, diapers, blankets, clothes, books, and computers?"

Carlos stared at me. "The baby's not even born. Why are you worrying about college?"

Then his sister came into the house with her brood,

and Carlos herded me toward our almost-finished room, making me walk backward.

"I'm a pregnant woman!" I said loudly. "I'm pregnant and I want a college savings account!"

Mariana pulled her children to her side.

Carlos backed me up the stairs.

Only glass was needed in the window frames, and a plumber to hook up the toilet and the hot water heater I'd purchased. But weeks had gone by. One plumber was busy. Another was a drunk and never showed up.

Carlos followed me up. "Glass, how hard is that?" I grumbled. He could never make me happy. I always wanted something else.

"I'll get it myself. I'll help my father put it in this weekend."

"That's what I need from you. This is what I need from you all the time." I was a señora now, with bossing rights.

Carlos nodded gravely. I gave him an awkward hug, my stomach in the way.

I should have let the moment be. But then I said, "And I want you to finish school."

I CAN'T STOP LOOKING AT HER

Maximo and Carlos spent weekends installing glass and hooking up the toilet. The hot water heater required a plumber. We moved in anyway.

We had curtains and a real tile floor. We had a tiny cold-water shower. We had a door that closed on our apartment. I had a job and a trouble-free pregnancy. Life, I could say, was pretty OK. Hot water would have made life downright excellent, but the latest plumber couldn't get his bicycle to work.

So I soaked up the quiet. In the mornings, I cuddled next to Carlos until the last possible moment, my breath making little clouds over the blankets until, in one quick motion, I got out of bed. I headed in unlaced sneakers and my terry bathrobe to the shower room.

The tile in the shower room was cold under my feet. I reminded myself for the five-hundredth time to buy a pair of rubber sandals. I turned on a feeble spray and, shivering one last time, removed my bathrobe and stashed it on a high concrete shelf to keep it dry. First I stuck a toe into the spray and when chills ceased to race through my body, I put the whole foot in, then, took it out to soap it up. I washed and rinsed my body, part by part, saving my head for last.

The cold water numbed my head. I shampooed quickly, bent over, aware of the cold air on my back. I rinsed; still bent over so cold drips would not run down my back. Wrapping my head in a towel did not stop the throbbing that had begun with the first splash of icy water on my head. I pulled my bathrobe back on, opened the door to even colder morning air and slipped still damp feet into my sneakers. Wind rattled the birdcages as I crossed the patio, ballooning the pain in my head to a full-blown headache. I blew my hair dry to warm my head, pulled on wool pants and took the bus into the center of town.

When I was ten, my life was perfect. My sister and I spent the summer racing each other across the Aronomink Swim Club pool. Our neighbor, Jeffrey Swan, was the lifeguard. Jeffrey's hair had bleached up like a rock star's but hormones hadn't turned us into lunatics yet. Other girls tied and retied the strings to their bikini tops below his wooden stand. But Jen and I dived off the high dive. We worked on our back and front flips. We sat on the hot concrete when we forgot our towels. We signed for French fries on our dad's tab.

In our almost-perfect life, Carlos and I ate on two chairs pulled up to the side of the bed. A small wicker crib trimmed in white eyelet and gauze sat next to the drop leaf desk. It held a small lacy white pillow and a white blanket—a collective gift from friends. Late in the day, the room was warm. Life almost felt normal, whatever that was anymore.

///

On December 22, I dialed my midwife, Alice's number. "I have news," I said when she answered.

"No, I have news."

"No, I have news. O.K. You first."

"Darlene had a boy last night," Alice said. I gasped.

"That's great! How's everybody?"

"Darlene's fine. The baby's fine. A boy. And I'm tired. What's your news?" I almost didn't have the heart.

"My water broke."

Alice and her husband arrived in their VW bug minutes later and we piled in. Carlos pulled my hastily packed overnight bag in after him.

"Darlene and Rick named their boy Harry Popocatepetl," Alice said. I looked at Carlos.

"The volcano erupted. México City is filled with smoke and ash," my husband explained. I should have been listening to the morning radio.

"Any contractions?" Alice asked.

"Nope."

Alice's husband lurched from the curb, and sped away as if he had seen too many pregnant lady-on-the-verge-in-the-back-of-the-taxi movies. Carlos took my hand and held on as if for life.

There is a photo of me wandering the hospital hall – which didn't have a door, only an open entryway – in a green gown and socks, and another of me lifting my gown to show I am wearing a diaper, ha-ha. And there is Carlos on a couch in the lounge, wearing olive pants and a black button down shirt, arms folded over his chest and looking as if someone just put a gun to his head. After the Pitocin kicked in, there weren't any more pictures.

The doctor brought in a back up team of two doctors and two nurses to tell the crazy American lady who wanted to do everything naturally that she needed a cesarean. "*Es que eres muy grande,*" they each said in turn. After all, you are quite old.

I was thirty six and already convinced, before they'd said a word, after five hours of laboring on my knees and vomiting into a bucket, that I did not want my baby inside of me one second longer.

"*Apurense!*" I said, waving an arm from the bedside, where I was bent over, cheek on the sheet, taking thirty seconds of rest before the next contraction hit me like a wave on a stormy day at the Jersey shore. Hurry up already! The doctors raised their eyebrows and hurried off to prepare the surgery salon.

I was out in space and there were angels all around me. One was holding my hand and she looked like Alice. Then a happy angel with a mustache said, "Do you want to see your baby?" and a tiny space creature zoomed over my head, bloody and blinking big brown eyes. How nice, somebody clean that puppy up and give me a blanket. Did I think it or say it? If I didn't get a blanket soon, somebody was going to pay. I had never been so cold in my life. Somebody had better stop that woodpecker noise in my head too. I tried to touch my face where my jaw hurt, but my arm seemed to belong to someone else; I couldn't make it move.

"They're stitching you up now. You'll be warm soon," Alice the angel soothed. She stroked the side of my cheek, and I realized my teeth were chattering so rapidly my face hurt. "Did you see? She's beautiful," Alice murmured. She? I hadn't noticed that part. I would check all the features as soon as they let me out of the block of ice they had me trapped in.

Blankets were piled on top of me and I was being wheeled through more space. All I could feel was grateful, grateful to be warm. I thought of toast and soup and hot chocolate and standing by the hot water heater in the basement of our house on Anderson Avenue in my snowsuit as my mother peeled off my mittens. It was nice here in space.

I didn't have to think about anything. They were taking me somewhere, but as long as I was warm along the way, I didn't care where it was. My ship must have had wheels— I heard them clackety-clacking underneath me. Then my blankets were being disturbed and a hand was grabbing and squeezing mine and I dropped from space, opening my eyes. Everything came into focus. Some closed doors came into sight. A wall clock read five to midnight. My husband's face appeared above me, wet, rapturous, trying to say many things. I could see there were a lot of words there, stuck behind his wide, flat cheekbones. Tears came out in their place until some words broke through.

"*Gracias por darme mi hija*. Thank you for giving me my daughter," my husband said, smiling a vulnerable, proud and frightened smile as if he had just realized the pregnancy had produced a living creature that would require his love and care. Then his face folded again and the words turned to rain. He wiped his cheek with the back of the hand that still held mine, our fingers interlaced, like some crazy bleached-out brown and white zebra or faded piano keys. I forgot to notice what color the baby was. I'd only seen a mucousy, blood-streaked being flying over my head. Dulce and Juana had speculated several times in the past months about the baby's color. "*Clarito*," they said in a desirous tone. Light-skinned. "Maybe it will have blue eyes," they said as well, as if that would be the ultimate, a charm for the dark-toned family, and what envy it would inspire among their neighbors to have a clear-eyed *guero* in their midst. Carlos had said he only wanted a healthy baby, the rest didn't matter. He held my hand to his chest now and kissed my forehead, my cheek.

The gurney came to a stop and a man in white pants and turtleneck lifted me from my wheeled ship. My husband slipped his arms under my legs and my back and together they moved me to the bed. "Blankets," I said before

I drifted into my first grade classroom where I was sitting next to the pinging radiator, the overhead lights bright because it was gray outside, almost like dinnertime, and snowing.

I had a child and I didn't know what she looked like! It was seven in the morning and I was fully present in the hospital room with peach and mint green curtains. There were boxes of pills on the bedside table and I was attached, by a needle and rubber tube, to a glass bottle hanging on a pole. My husband slept, open-mouthed, on a bench against the wall, covered only with his jacket. I sat up, feeling the strange, flaccid, bulgeless skin below my breasts and pulled my bathrobe on one-armed. I drove the pole over to the wall bench and touched Carlos' shoulder.

"Carlos, go get in the bed," I whispered. His eyes flew open. He looked like he was coming back from space, where I had been.

"I just fell asleep. They sent me out to get drugs for you. I spent the rest of the night looking at the baby."

"I'm going to go see her. Get in the bed."

"You can't..."

"I'm fine." I pointed at the bed, but Carlos dropped back to sleep as I stood there, without having moved anything but his eyeballs. I took a blanket and put it over him.

There were two babies in cradles shrouded in white mosquito netting in the nursery. One, a boy, had deep brown skin like my father's wing tips and a huge head of midnight black hair like my husband's. There was black hair growing down his cheeks like Elvis sideburns, and I saw hair on his arms, too, when I peeked under the blankets. Maybe that's what Carlos looked like when he was a baby, I reasoned. He turned out handsome.

The other baby was the color of *café-con-leche*. She had a lovely round face and hardly any hair at all. She looked at me from enormous brown eyes laced with long, graceful eyelashes like my sister's. I looked at the bassinets' name-plates, hoping for the pretty baby, already telling myself I could love the hairy one. Ortega Baby it said in black magic marker at the feet of the cow-eyed, coffee-and-cream-colored girl. She was mine.

The final photo is off-color. Carlos didn't want to startle the baby with the flash so it is taken in natural light. I am wearing the same wide smock-top I wore into the hospital. I am half-lying on the bench where Carlos slept, looking at the bundle next to me. A perfectly formed face shows from the blankets, the delicate, translucent eyelids closed. "Look here," Carlos commanded, camera to his face. But I can't. Only the side of my face is visible in the photo, and my arm around the bundle. I can't stop looking at her.

///

At the top of the hill I held the baby, dizzied by the perfection of her head, the way her body curled as if it were still in mine, and her size—I could have placed her in one of my father's sneakers.

I started down the rocky hill, holding the baby close, walking gingerly to protect my stitched-up abdomen. Carlos extended his arms, but I held the bundle tighter and picked my way down the washed-out trail.

Dulce saw us from the doorway and came running, leaping over rocks, yelling over her shoulder that *ya llego el bebe*. Carlos and I stared mute as my sister-in-law took the baby from my arms and ran back down the hill with her toward the house.

My husband took a few steps and looked back at me impatiently. I felt nothing but the cold wind on my cheeks and the emptiness of my arms. Finally, my husband took my hand, and I allowed him to lead me around the sticker bushes and down the hill.

Exclamations of delight could be heard from the house and Carlos hurried inside. I walked behind him, furiously, alone.

Inside, Dulce held the pink blanket back so Juana could see my baby, and I saw how it would be—the two ladies who spent their lives caring for infants taking over the child's care. I held my arms out. Dulce looked at me with a you-don't-know-anything-about-babies look, then when I didn't lower my arms, slowly handed my daughter back. I inhaled my daughter's delicate newborn smell, an aroma still mixed with the odor of my own body.

ESCAPE

There was an afternoon tea at Darlene and Rick's eleven days after Carla's birth and I had already tried on my old Levi's and found, with some squeezing, they fit. I wanted to speak in English with other adults. I wanted to see their baby, Harry Popocatepetl, and show off Carla. I needed to escape my mother-in-law, who tried to prevent me from going outside.

"Don't go," Carlos said.

"If I don't get out of this house, I will jump right out of my skin," I growled. "Why don't you come with me?"

"My mother says it's bad for the baby to go out in the cold."

"I was born in December. My mother took me out right away. I survived!"

"My Gerónimo was born in May, the hottest month. I stayed in for my forty days and you better believe I wanted to go out and find some water to cool off in," said Juana from the doorway. How had I not heard her enter? "*Hace daño el aire,"* she said with conviction. How could outside arm do any harm, and what was the difference between outside air and inside air in a house that barely had any doors?

I unfolded a pink fleecy Winnie-the-Pooh cold-weather suit with feet, and checked my purse for taxi change.

"Susana, it's going to do *you* damage to go out," Juana said in an I-know-best voice. "You shouldn't be walking, much less carrying the baby."

Carla opened her mouth as I zipped her into the Winnie-the-Pooh suit. "Let's make a break for it and I'll feed you at Darlene and Rick's," I whispered.

"Sue," my husband said. I looked him in the eye.

"You go off every day with your brother and I sit here! Imagine yourself not leaving this house for ten days. I'm home every day now and I see you less than when I was pregnant." I yanked on my coat. "I am not doing anything to harm your baby. I am going to drink tea in Darlene and Ted's nice warm house and come home in a taxi." I walked through the house as fast I could. Little pains shot through my lower belly reminding me I had been recently opened and stitched back up again.

"*Tápala!*" Juana called in a near-hysterical voice as I passed the kitchen. Juana was lifting a pot using two tortillas as oven mitts. I covered the baby's body with a blanket and threw the top of it over my shoulder, making a little tent over her face like the Mexican women did. I walked out the door, feeling the January wind on my cheeks like a rush of freedom. I saw Juana watching me from our bay window, then felt Carlos at my side, pulling a jacket on. I smiled at the taxi driver who stopped for us at the drainpipe, suddenly jubilant. My husband had defied his mother. He was with me.

///

Carlos got a job as a waiter's assistant. He started the day I flew to Philadelphia to show off Carla.

I read a parenting magazine on the plane. "Your baby won't stop crying and you want to run away but you can't— you have a nine o'clock meeting!" an article screeched. Nowhere were there articles about your sister-in-law giving you red string to tie around the baby's wrist to ward off evil spirits.

"Don't pay any attention to Mariana," Carlos had said. "Her husband's brother was going out with another woman and the wife got a *bruja* to witch him. They say that's why he got diabetes."

The string was in my pocket. I touched it now and then. What harm could it do?

After eight days, I arrived back in Mexico City loaded with presents. Carlos met me and took my bags. We walked past the ladies toilet in the bus station, where an ancient woman threw a bucket of water down the loo after you used it. Carlos handed me a torta, wrapped in a napkin. Juggling food, bags and baby, we boarded the Flecha Amarilla to San Miguel.

Carlos settled Carla in the crook of his arm.

"Look." I unzipped the sports bag my father had given me and showed him cookies in tin foil, muffins, baby books, clothes for a six-month-old, and clothes for when she was a year.

"Hmm," he said, nodding. He only had eyes for Carla. "You can't take her away for that long again," he sighed. Carlos nuzzled her nose with his. Lulled by the bus, we leaned our heads together on the seat.

In Juana's house, I kicked a crumpled Sabritas potato chips bag in the entrance hall and pushed aside a ball of wire that might have tangled my feet and pitched me head-first to the floor with my baby in my arms if I hadn't seen it. A banana peel peeked from the planter near the stairs; a wad of chewed gum showed pink in the dirt in another. I rewrapped my rebozo and fussed at some invisible drool on Carla's chin, trying to calm myself. I thought I was fighting the urge to vomit but realized what was pushing into my throat was despair. My mother's house was pristine – anti-bacterialized surfaces everywhere. Suddenly I could barely stand to have my feet on the sticky floor.

I hurried up to our room, plopped myself in the rocking chair, and lifted my shirt. In the corners of the room, dust had gathered in triangular clumps. There was dust in the un-mortared grooves on the floor too, and crumbs. A film coated the lamp next to the bed and I could have written my name on the top of the television. I tilted my head back in the rocker so my tears would not fall on the baby feeding at my breast. Was this all I had to offer her?

Carlos was in the doorway when I opened my eyes.

"How's your job?" I asked, wiping my nose on the inside hem of my shirt.

"I quit."

"What?"

"I hated it. The customers are arrogant. They talk to you as if you are a burro. 'Get this. Bring me bread.' And the manager is a nervous wreck. He's going to kill if you don't bring the guy who is yelling at you a glass of water."

"When did you quit?"

"The day you left." He picked a hangnail. "I went to Celaya on the bus and paid the rest of the hospital bill."

"That's good," I said dully. "What did you do for two weeks?"

"I missed you."

What was love anyway? I closed my eyes. I wanted to sleep a long, deep sleep.

///

The next month, Carlos and I took the bus downtown with Carla. Carlos had an appointment to show the magnets and boxes he was making to a store. When he went in, I sat on a Jardín bench, dreaming of having enough income to rent our own place. I pointed to the pigeons and Carla watched them with Betty Boop eyes.

"Oh," said an American lady stopping in front of me. I recognized her as an artist who'd drawn me in my modeling days. "I didn't know you had a baby."

"Usually, when I'm downtown, she's at home with my mother-in-law."

"How lucky you are! Mexican children never cry. They are so well behaved on the street. Mexican families stay together."

I was used to this by now – the desperate romanticizing of Mexican family life. I didn't argue. I could have said, hey, I have a sister-in-law who studied law in León. She only did two years though. Then she had to come home to prepare her father's meals. I could have said, my husband dotes on me, but he's a bit of a youngster who doesn't want to leave his mother, who, no matter what he accomplishes or doesn't, always has a hot plate of food for him. It's the goal of the Mexican mother, you see, I could have gone on, to keep her sons at home. It's not mine though, I would have continued. No siree. Living out my life in Mexico with the in-laws is not my goal at all.

NINETY-DOLLAR APARTMENT

"It's right downtown. It has a patio and a hot water heater and it's available at the beginning of next month." I faced my husband in our small room, the blue walls stained now with a white deodorant splash from when a roll-on ball had flown off once. The bathroom window was still covered with thick purple plastic sheeting. I'd given up on making improvements months before, hoarding my money for flight.

"An apartment downtown to be close to the book-store," I said. My old modeling friend, Claudia had opened a bookstore, and I had a job there.

"My mother's house is closer to the prepa."

I placed my hand on my lower belly where a second baby grew. "*Four* of us in this house?"

Carlos shrugged. He'd grown up like that – he and five sisters and brothers all in one room.

He pulled from his pocket a pink receipt. September 1995. *Pagado*.

"You're going back to school?"

"I'm going to finish."

"A step in the right direction." I dangled a Virgen de Guadalupe keychain from my finger. It had a house key on it. "Now I want you to move with me."

///

I dressed Carla in a blue dress with a ruffled underskirt for her second birthday and blew up balloons and set cupcakes out on an oilcloth-covered table on the patio of our apartment. Carla's gift from us was a sister, born in a problem-free home birth in the downtown apartment of a midwife trainee I'd met the afternoon my labor pains started. Sean Paula was born one day before Carla turned two in December. On her real birthday, I spent the day drinking all the liquids I could find in bed in the midwife's house, breastfeeding the infant. And then I was recovering, and then there was one more Christmas with our fake foot-high tree in the window of the apartment in the lamina-roofed house, a fact that would have depressed me if it weren't for the deep contentment of having our new baby girl in my arms. So Carla's birthday came and went.

While I didn't make my goal of leaving Juana and Maximo's house before Christmas, I did in the spring. Secretly I had to admit that it was better that way after all—having Juana's help with two very small children in the first months. I didn't fret about not having toys or baby utensils the second time around. I had decided Carla hadn't missed them at all. Carla had spent her infanthood tucked into my mother-in-law's rebozo. She rode face-out at Juana's bosom, watching the world from a secure vantage point, included in everything. When tired, she slept right on my mother-in-law's breast too, or in the cradle Juana fashioned by tying a sheet to a roof beam. I was glad Sean could spend her first six months in Juana's rebozo too.

Now were in our own place.

Gussie's boyfriend, Toño, had been awarded a grant to study cactuses and they had moved, leaving us their ninety-dollar a month apartment. It was small but had a fireplace and a roomy kitchen and was close to everything, especially the bookstore where I still worked. We were in our own place.

We had space, and we were throwing Carla her birthday party. Paper *picado* flags crisscrossed the kitchen. Claudia from the bookstore came and Alice and Gussie, visiting from Mexico City. Carlos poured *agua de jamaica* into paper cups for the guests.

"Carlos, look," I whispered, as Juana came up the stairs wearing a skirt and carrying a cake box. "Did your mother ever give you a cake for your birthday?"

"Never."

"Think I'm rubbing off on her?"

"We never had a trash can in the house until you moved in. And now my mother takes vitamins. What do you think?"

"Carla, come and see what your Tita brought," I called into the house. "Juana, thank you so much." I took the box and put out paper plates. "Yum, es de tres leches," I announced, opening the box. A three-milks-cake. Maximo insisted that the cake was made with cow, goat and burro milk. Next to the cake was the fifty-dollar German knife I'd given Juana to save her hands more than a year ago.

Juana bustled into the kitchen and, pulling a large bag of tamales from her market bag, looked for a pan in which to heat them. But this was my house.

"*Venga*," I said. I showed my mother-in-law to a chair at the head of the table. Carla pushed a plastic three-wheeler up to her grandmother. Juana looked around, surprised to be seated. Carlos brought her a cup of juice, and she sat back and laughed.

FAMILY REUNION

It's almost fall in the Atlantic Seaboard and we are in a McDonald's just off Route 9, the four of us—myself, Carlos, Carla and Sean Paula. It is supposed to be a riotous occasion—a first trip to the iconic fast food joint for my foreign-born family! But instead of guiding them through this American moment with grace, I am screaming and throwing a Coke loaded with ice at a trashcan.

Carlos grabs all the wrappers on the table with one hand and stuffs them into the same trash can, holding Sean, our second daughter, in his other arm. One-handed, he stacks the trays.

Over by the door, I'm tapping my foot. "I hate air-conditioning. Don't you? Look. Goosebumps on my arms. It's not even hot. It's September, for Chrissake."

Carla is still at the booth we occupied, pushing French fries into her mouth. Carlos fast-walks back—people move out of his way—and scoops her from the bench.

In the car, he takes the driver's side.

"You don't have a U.S. license."

"Ni modo."

The car air conditioner hums on as the car turns over and I snap it off.

"You have to tell them," my husband says tersely. "As soon as we get back."

We are staying at my parents' New Jersey shore house for a large family reunion. There are 24-packs of beer and giant Tupperware containers of potato and macaroni salad in the extra refrigerator in the garage. I have met Paul's one-year old son for the first time, and he, our girls. Bill's daughter is eight. Jen has brought Christopher, the financial whiz boyfriend up from Washington D.C. and my mother is being extra nice. Christopher has the kind of hairline that tells you in ten years he'll be bald. He hovers around Jen like she's a prize, running to the drug store for her, carrying her bag and chair to the beach.

"Later. Too many people around now."

Uncle Len is doing dinner—his famous crab and shrimp boil. That means he calls Marie's Fish Restaurant on the bay and orders it up.

"Susie, come on!" Uncle Len calls later in the afternoon, as I snap through the pages of one of my mother's cookbooks. He motions me toward his car, cans of Schlitz bulging from each back pocket. He pops one for me and cranks the car into gear. "Nice looking guy you got there, eh. Seems decent."

"Decent. Yes, he's that."

Carlos and I have weathered three years in the ninety-dollar apartment. We've sailed through high school graduation and the start of a new business. We give massages and facials. We have two employees and four tables. We are real spa owners. What else was there for a writer and an artist to do? An architect has just finished the design for the house we'll build. We have starter money from my parents.

Back in Juana's house, the hot water heater is finally connected. She and Maximo moved to the upstairs room when we left. Hugo married a pretty local girl who is about to have their first child. At their wedding, an American hippie Hugo knew from the basketball courts played Beatles songs on his guitar. Hugo and Marisol live in the downstairs room in Juana's house. Hugo goes back and forth to León, finishing his degree to be a physical education teacher. Carlos is four years away from enrolling in college. Meantime, he speaks English to clients and gives massage that have people melting into chairs when he's done.

Our future is bright yet I can't sleep at night, my fingernails are ragged and my kids have begun to be careful around me. I'm in therapy, uncovering buried anger. No, not buried. It's right there on the surface, ready to erupt all over the people closest to me with the slightest provocation. My therapist won't let me back in to see her if I don't tell my parents what happened all those years ago after Kareem Abdul Jabbar's birthday party. I know she's right. I'm so over the silence. It has made my family wonder why I have had such a chip on my shoulder. It has stopped me from saying so many things to my parents. It's made me a big fat fake when I'm around most people. Still, I'd rather give birth a thousand times, have a disfiguring skin disease, suffer an eye twitch for life than have this talk.

We eat beefsteak tomatoes and boiled shrimp and clams for dinner, sopping up clam juice with baguettes, which in South Jersey are just called hard rolls. My father has found a piñata, a *gusanito verde*. A happy green worm. It swings from a rope over the front yard.

After dinner, my mother, sister and sisters-in-law and I pick up the paper plates as our girls line up with their American cousins for a turn at whacking the green worm. Carlos gently spins Bill's daughter, Chloe. When he steps back, my mother drapes an arm over Carlos' shoulder.

Finally the piñata is broken, candy is scooped, and my relatives go back to their beach rentals, or to the bars. Carlos and I go upstairs in my parents' house to put the kids to bed.

"Breathe," Carlos says. He is rubbing Carla's back and I am pacing between the twin beds. Sean is asleep, swimsuit still on beneath her shorts. Carlos holds up a hand—Carla is asleep too.

Carlos nods at me. I stop. I hear Tom Brokaw below. My husband takes my hand, looks me in the eye. "You can do this."

I have written a letter. I will just read it to them. Downstairs, I face them, text in hand, and say I have something to tell them.

"Uh-oh," my mother says.

But I start crying with huge gulps and I can't. I crumple the letter, stuff it in my pocket and collapse onto the floral couch. My parents sit rigidly on either side of me. Finally I get the words out—all of them.

"What an ass," my father hisses about the agent who called me. "He ripped off a lot of his players and then one by one, they all fired him. Not a good person. Honey, honey, I am sorry that happened to you."

I put my head on his chest and his arms go around me. I cry and cry and he lets me.

My mother is fighting to hug me now. My father releases me.

"Sue, I am so sorry." My mother takes my hands in hers. "I am so sorry I didn't notice. I was so out of it that whole year, so focused on getting your dad well that I barely noticed you kids. I think you all suffered."

I'm hiccupping into not weeping, but my mother looks as if she will.

"Mom, don't cry. We're all fine. And you did keep Dad alive." My siblings and I believe it.

My dad clears his throat. "I'm sorry I was in a coma and couldn't defend you." It's not very funny but we all laugh a little bit. Life is so absurd: my father's accident, my marriage, my mother, worrying through it all. Was there a right path for any of us that would have led to less hardship? Would we have traded any of it? Probably not, because our choices and circumstances have led to this—us on a couch in New Jersey with the salty aroma of the bay wafting in through the screen door and our arms around each other.

My father shifts on the couch, glad to have lightened the moment. I get up and sit on the footstool and look at them. My wonderful parents, who got a piñata to add something Mexican to the party, who have only wanted the best for me always.

"Hey," my father says. He nods his head up the stairs. There at the top are Carlos' sneakers, the rest of him hidden in darkness.

"Go on up," my father says, and I do, my heart soaring ahead of me.

2010

Carlos and I are both a tiny bit crinkly around the eyes now. I still have a sprinkle of freckles on my cheeks and a runner's butt. We sit in the Jardín bench on a Sunday night, watching the paseo.

The promenade is madly informal now, but still happening. The nineties are over and the girls wear skirts again. They clutch each other's arms and walk, eyeing the boys. The boys shoulder each other and say, "*No seas pendejo, guey,*" when the girls walk by. Don't be a moron, dude. Their jostling scatters a bobbing gaggle of pigeons. Adults eat ice cream cones and watch the flirting from Jardín benches.

That's us across from the elote seller, trying to be invisible and not offend our own teens. Sean, at 13, is two inches taller than I am and model-slender. It's hard to sway her from her general outlook that 13-year old boys are witless. The best of the male species, according to Sean, is her horse, Andale. Rather than eyeing boys, Sean angles to get change from her parents for a Starbucks while trying to look as if she's not related to us.

Carla, at 15, has McKinney freckles and Ortega curves. She is horse crazy, too, and needs a boy to live up to the undying loyalty of her horse, Lucky. The only promenading Carla would be interested in would be a victory lap on Lucky after winning a dressage competition.

Mariachis in studded pants sing *Cielito Lindo* under the portales. Carlos drops the last of his cone for the pigeons, and puts out his hand. I take it, and we walk to the elote seller. There, Carlos drops my hand and by my elbow, turns me toward Calle Correo. "You go that way," he says, and I walk away without looking back, knowing I'll see him on the other side.

///

ACKNOWLEDGEMENTS

First, I thank my true blue writing pals, *mis compañeras*, Beverly Donofrio and Sandra Gulland. My gratitude for their professional help to Lauda Fields, Fred Hills, Laura Fraser, Lisa Coleman, Carol and Larry Rand, Johanna Moran, Mina Rollin Will, and the San Miguel Literary Sala. And, *gracias* to special family members for their endearing support—Jack and Claire McKinney and Ann McKinney Holtby.

SPANISH GLOSSARY OF COMMON EXPRESSIONS

andale: Go on. Go ahead. Go.
azucar: Sugar
bolillo: Sandwich roll
caldo: Broth
chispas: (Literally, sparks) Gee whiz.
fresa: (Literally, strawberry) Entitled rich kid. Preppie.
molcajete: Flat grinding board made of volcanic stone
nada: Nothing
ni modo: It doesn't matter.
pinche: Darn, damn, blasted
quien sabe: Who knows?
Quinceaños: Fifteenth year
ropa vieja: Old clothes
Ya me voy: I'm going now.

WORDS TO USE WHEN "FLIRTING IN SPANISH"

amor: Love
beso: A kiss
coquetear: To flirt
esposa: Wife
marido: Husband
novio: Boyfriend
novia: Girlfriend

SLIGHTLY CURSI (SMARMY OR TACKY) NAMES CAN CALL YOUR SWEETHEART

Cariño: Dear
Corazón: Heart
Mi amor: My love
Mi vida: My life
Mi cielo: My sky or my everything
Mi reina/rey: My queen/king
Mi tesoro: My treasure
Muñeca: Doll
Nena/nene: Baby

WHAT YOU CAN SAY TO YOUR TRUE LOVE

Estoy loco por ti: I'm crazy about you.
Te necesito: I need you.
Te quiero: I want you. I love you.
Te amo: I love you.
No quiero vivir sin ti: I can't live without you.
Bésame: Kiss me.
Abrázame: Hug me.
Te extraño, te echo de menos: I miss you.

ؤؤؤ

UN DICHO MEXICANO – A MEXICAN SAYING

Donde fuego hubo cenizas quedan: Where there was fire, ashes remain. An old love may be rekindled.

CPSIA information can be obtained
at www.ICGtesting.com
Printed in the USA
BVHW031409120620
581249BV00003B/73

9 780982 859193